SCARED
TO LIFE

Finding Courage in a Scary World

D1175488

CONTENTS

DEDICATION AND ACKNOWLEDGMENTS

This book is dedicated to those who journey in fear. May you find yourself in the protective arms of your Creator as you gather courage for each step. May you find your identity, value, and destiny as the foundation of your inspiration. Go make the world less scary for those who follow you.

Thank you to my wife for your support and contribution to this work as well as my entire life. I thank God for the partner he has given me. Thank you to Janet Blakely for your tireless desire to see writers blossom to their full potential. Thank you to Dee-Dee Franklin for your design skill and expertise. And thank you to all those scared people who gave me the privilege of helping them walk in courage through life's storms.

INTRODUCTION

Each morning I walked to the bus stop where my friends gathered to wait for the yellow machine to deliver us safely to school. The driver usually greeted me with a smile. I walked up the steps and found a window seat as the bus bounded along the route. Soon a familiar dread would overtake my heart as fear gripped my spirit approaching Roger's stop. For some unknown reason, Roger bullied me incessantly. Was it my stunning good looks or sharp wit? I know not.

Roger wasn't one for high-level conversation, so I never knew why. He was good at intimidation, pressure, and all the qualities that make one a good bully. In places where I should have felt safe, on the bus and at school, I found myself dodging fear. Maybe your life is like that. Fear chases you.

Fear and anxiety account for most of the mental and emotional disorders of our day.[1] These often affect the young among us.

The World Health Organization (WHO) released a new set of stats on teen mental health—and the numbers are staggering . . .
- Half of all mental health conditions start by the age of 14.

---

1. Anxiety Disorders—Facts and Statistics, Accessed March 27, 2020. https://adaa.org/about-adaa/press-room/facts-statistics.

- Suicide is the third leading cause of death in 15-19-year-olds.

Fear and mental health struggles affect teens around the world—and maybe even in your own home.[2] While we could drone on with statistics, what matters most to me is you. If you're reading this book, you must have some interest in overcoming fear in a healthy, holistic way. That's what this book is about.

Fear can be a healthy emotion that signals danger ahead. Or it can be a tyrannical slave master that debilitates your life and reduces you to a shell of the person God designed you to be.

There—I said it—"God." God is often a polarizing word. It divides worldviews and perspectives. This book acknowledges God as your designer and your redeemer. Without him in the world, we should be scared and depressed; for then, this world is all there is. No meaning, no purpose, just "blind, pitiless indifference."[3]

But we long for purpose; we long for meaning. We have no longing for which there is no satisfaction. We thirst and find water. We hunger and locate food. We long for meaning hoping to discover a grand story. We yearn for purpose, supposing a design for our lives. A story must have a storyteller. A design must have a designer. As C.S. Lewis stated in *Mere Christianity,* "If I find

---

2. Adolescent Mental Health, March 28, 2020. https://www.who.int/news-room/fact-sheets/detail/adolescent-mental-health.

3. Atheist Richard Dawkins wrote in his book, *The Blind Watchmaker* on p. 133: "The universe we observe has precisely the properties we should expect if there is, at bottom, no design, no purpose, no evil, no good, nothing but blind, pitiless indifference."

in myself desires which nothing in this world can satisfy, the only logical explanation is that I was made for another world."

In this book, we point you to the One who calms the sea and stills the anxious heart. While I give you more tools than just religious platitudes, without a connection to the One who can redeem all wrong, my advice would be infinitely incomplete.

I draw on more than fifty years of living in a scary world, including over thirty years pastoring people through fear-inducing circumstances. I'm grateful to clinicians who have helped me learn liberating knowledge. In addition, I can look back over thirty years as a flight instructor helping people function in times of stress and legitimate fear.

I look forward to seeing how God will help you grow, liberate you, and use you to help rescue others from the tyrants of fear and anxiety.

Godspeed,
Carey Waldie

CHAPTER ONE
You Should Be Scared

It was a wonderful November morning at the airport in Anchorage, Alaska. Air traffic moved smoothly without delay. The controllers in the twelve-story tower communicated a sequence for landing to each inbound aircraft. Then it happened. A 7.0 magnitude earthquake violently shook the tower. The controllers perched over a hundred feet in the air held on to anything stable. A controller at a neighboring air base said, "You just kind of feel like your time's up. You just start thinking like, 'Goodbye wife, goodbye kids, this stinks.' That kind of stuff. Very life or death kind of thoughts come in pretty quickly."

The airplanes still lined up for landing, remained oblivious to the plight on the ground until one controller, able to steady himself enough blurted out across the radio, "Fed-Ex, go around! Fed-Ex, go around!"[4] The pilots, only feet from landing, called back confused, "Was that for Fed-Ex?" Then silence from the tower. The pilot inquired, "Tower, Fed-Ex 49?" "Fed-Ex 49 heavy

---

4. You can listen to the audio here:
https://www.youtsube.com/watch?v=o80cNJ_XhX0&t=38s&ab_channel=VASAviation-

go around!" came the reply. The pilot advanced the throttle on his million-pound aircraft and lifted it toward the sky again.

Confusion, fear, and panic—all these emotions boiled around for a time after the earthquake. Controllers evacuated the tower and set up shop in the back of a Ford pickup. Pilots orbited until ground crews determined the runways were safe from buckles and folds. Landing a large jet on a buckled runway at one hundred and twenty miles per hour would spell instant disaster. Life is normal and enjoyable—then suddenly the earth begins to shake. When what you think is stable, reliable, and steady begins to shake, the world can be a scary place. *Fear is normal when what you count on to steady you becomes unstable.*

FEAR IS NORMAL WHEN WHAT YOU COUNT ON TO STEADY YOU BECOMES UNSTABLE.

RECIPE FOR FEAR

Why, with all our modern conveniences and scientific advancements have we become so afraid? I believe we have created a world in which the solid foundations of life have begun to move. The lighthouses we used to look to for bearings now float around the oceans of our lives making nothing certain. We've arrived at this point through a confluence of events and worldview shifts, including:

1. The disconnect from the transcendent
2. The disintegration of the family
3. 24-hour global news cycle
4. 24-hour comparison through social media
5. Increased isolation

DISCONNECT FROM THE TRANSCENDENT

Transcendent means the world beyond physical human experience. It means reaching into the world beyond you. We've been told that ultimate reality is simply the material world. "We have outgrown our need for God," they say. "We've been to the moon and invented the internet, why do we need God?" This attitude has cost us.

Psychoanalyst Erica Komisar, writing to parents in the Wall Street Journal asserts,

As a therapist, I'm often asked to explain why depression and anxiety are so common among children and adolescents. One of the most important explanations—and perhaps the most neglected—is declining interest in religion. This cultural shift already has proved disastrous for millions of vulnerable young people.[5]

She cited a Harvard study of 5,000 children and teens:

Children or teens who reported attending a religious service at least once per week scored higher on psychological well-being measurements and had lower risks of mental illness. Weekly attendance was associated with higher rates of volunteering, a sense of mission, forgiveness, and lower probabilities of drug use and early sexual initiation.

Disconnecting ourselves from the foundation of our existence causes the world to shake, resulting in corresponding fear, nihilism, and depression.

THE DISINTEGRATION OF THE FAMILY

So many people have felt the pain and uncertainty of a family that has disintegrated. The family is designed to be a safe place. When this foundation begins to quake, the world becomes a scary place. A flood of "what if's" dominates your thinking. When

5. Erica Komisar, Don't Believe in God? Lie to Your Children, Accessed July 19, 2022. https://www.wsj.com/articles/dont-believe-in-god-lie-to-your-children-11575591658

a family breaks, a story ends—not happily. While new stories begin, the pain and trauma often color the new stories.

The family works best when there's a mom and a dad. Hundreds of sociological studies have shown this. The Heritage think tank found that only 11 percent of American children lived apart from their dads in 1960. Today, the number has grown to 27 percent—nearly one in three.

"There is a "father absence crisis in America," according to the National Fatherhood Initiative, and the results are sobering.

Studies have found that children raised without a father are:

- At a higher risk of having behavioral problems
- Four times more likely to live in poverty
- More likely to be incarcerated in their lifetime
- Twice as likely to never graduate high school
- At a seven times higher risk of teen pregnancy
- More vulnerable to abuse and neglect
- More likely to abuse drugs and alcohol
- Twice as likely to be obese

From education to personal health to career success, children who lack a father find themselves at a disadvantage to their peers raised in a two-parent household.[6,7]

---

6. Accessed March 28, 2020.
https://www.fatherhood.org/father-absence-statistic .
7. Accessed March 28, 2020.
https://www.heritage.org/marriage-and-family/commentary/the-importance-dads-increasingly-fatherless-america.

24-HOUR GLOBAL NEWS

Growing up, I had access to about three channels. (I say "about" because depending on how well the antenna worked, you might get PBS.) Each night at the same time newscasters like Walter Cronkite would tell us "The way it is." That's it. For thirty minutes a day we could see what was happening in the world.

It all changed with cable TV. In June 1980, Ted Turner founded Cable News Network (CNN) just in time for a war against Iraq—the first one. We could now view the news twenty-four hours a day. Today with the internet we can view all manner of hideous, heinous, and disturbing things with the click of a mouse.

It has now become rather obvious that news is not about informing people with unbiased reporting. The news is about ratings, eyeballs, and advertising dollars. Because of this bias—and the human desire to slow down and gawk at car crashes—the media know that to gain viewers they must pump the bad news. They say, "If it bleeds, it leads." So, if the story includes strife, death, calamity, and trauma, they will pump it to the front of the paper, newscast, and social media feed.

The result of sensationalized media saturating our lives creates a narrative in our head that includes:

- Unsafe neighborhoods and communities
- A belief that crime rates are rising

- Overestimating our odds of becoming a victim
- A belief that the world is a dangerous place.[8]

SOCIAL MEDIA COMPARISON AND ISOLATION

Our digital connection has blessed us with opportunity for social connection, but it has come with its own consequences. We have become curators of our own public relations empire. We can carefully craft our moments for that perfect post. When we compare ourselves with the perfect world of others, we find ourselves falling short. This breeds anxious hearts.

Ironically, the opportunity for *more* digital interaction has led to less *actual personal* connection. San Francisco State University Professor of Health Education Erik Peper, and Associate Professor of Health Education Richard Harvey surveyed 135 students and found that "Students who used their phones the most reported higher levels of feeling isolated, lonely, depressed, and anxious. They believe the loneliness is partly a consequence of replacing face-to-face interaction

---

8. Debora Serani, *"If It Bleeds, It Leads: Understanding Fear-Based Media,"* Accessed March 28, 2020. https://www.psychologytoday.com/us/blog/two-takes-depression/201106/if-it-bleeds-it-leads-understanding-fear-based-media.

with a form of communication where body language and other signals cannot be interpreted."[9]

Like all new technology, humans have found positive and negative ways to use it. The increased *positive* social interaction comes with increased *negative* social interaction including sexual pressure and cyberbullying. Now Roger can follow you off the bus into your home and relentlessly badger, harass, and intimidate you. Who wouldn't be anxious?

HOPE

The world we live in can be scary, but fear need not run your life. There is hope. God designed you to make a difference in this world. In the next few chapters, we will show you how to rise above your anxieties to accomplish what God designed you to do on this planet. The first step is to choose your scary and place all your hopes, dreams, and fears into his hands.

9. Lisa Owens Viani, "*Digital addiction increases loneliness, anxiety and depression*," Accessed March 28, 2020. https://news.sfsu.edu/news-story/digital-addiction-increases-loneliness-anxiety-and-depression.

THE WORLD CAN BE SCARY, BUT
FEAR NEED NOT RUN YOUR LIFE.
THERE IS HOPE. GOD DESIGNED YOU
TO MAKE A DIFFERENCE IN
THIS WORLD.

CHAPTER TWO
Your Friend, Scary Jesus

Bryan. I have no idea why he began picking on me. He was an oversized lug who enjoyed spitting on things. Weird, I know. Maybe it was my good looks and attractive charm but for whatever reason this kid found me appealing. He stole my things—including my new watch—and pushed me around. His presence created a lot of fear in my heart.

I weighed my options. I could respond with a direct attack. He was twice my size, and I had no fighting experience—so I ruled that out. I could set his car or house on fire. (I had lots of fire experience making my own gunpowder with a chemistry set for about four years at this point.) But I felt that might have some unintended consequences.

I decided I had only one option. I needed to find someone bigger and stronger than Bryan and make him my friend. I found him in Dave Peden. Dave was a mountain of a man whose legend included being a State Cop or Navy Seal or something. Anyway, he worked for the school. I told him my plight and Mr. Peden brought Bryan and I together for a peace summit that resulted in Bryan giving my stuff back and leaving me alone.

This peace wasn't a result of Bryan suddenly becoming a decent human being. (Bryan, if you're reading this, congratulations on your literacy.) It was the force of a larger, more powerful, and scarier person in my corner who vowed to be my advocate.

If you want to stop fear from bullying you and overcome paralyzing anxiety, you must choose your scary. You cannot eliminate fear. So you must choose *what you will fear. You must look for the biggest, scariest, and most powerful friend you can find.* That friend is Jesus.

JESUS: SCARY GOOD

When asked to give a list of the scariest people in the world, most people would not list the historical Jesus at the top, but his disciples would. They had first-hand experience with this terrifying man.

In Mark chapter four, we are given an account of Jesus and the disciples crossing the sea of Galilee. The geography in the region lends itself to sudden storms. As they crossed, a storm rushed across the water and waves began to crash over the boat. The disciples feared for their lives. Jesus, meanwhile, slept in the stern of the boat. The disciples, like kids in a thunderstorm, woke up Jesus saying to him, "Teacher, don't you care if we drown?"

20

Have you ever so needed sleep that you tried to get a few minutes of quiet? You lay down and almost instantly you found yourself in the most deep and dreamy and delicious sleep? Then someone in your life decided that their issue was more important than your wonderful nap. How did you feel as you awoke? A bit agitated I would guess.

I imagine Jesus woke up with a bit of an edge. I would not have wanted to be the storm. Mark relates in verse 39, "He got up, rebuked the wind and said to the waves, 'Quiet! Be still!' Then the wind died down and it was completely calm." Instantly the storm changed from raging to peace! The waves themselves retreated into the abyss and now the sea reflected the sky like glass.

He then turned his attention to the disciples, "Why are you so afraid? Do you still have no faith?" After this rebuke by Jesus, the disciples had a curious reaction. During the storm they experienced fear. After Jesus calmed the storm, Mark notes, "They were terrified . . ." The King James version translates it, "They feared exceedingly."

The storm was scary, but the man in the boat with them demonstrated power *greater* than the storm! The waves threatened to sink the ship. Jesus could sink the *universe!* And they couldn't get away, they were trapped in a boat with the most powerful man in the universe. To "fear exceedingly" is the natural response. "They were terrified and asked each other, 'Who is this? Even the wind and the waves obey him!'"

21

When the wind and the waves of life bring fear into your life, you must find someone scarier and stronger than the storm and make him your friend.

WHEN THE WIND AND WAVES OF LIFE BRING FEAR INTO YOUR LIFE, YOU MUST FIND SOMEONE SCARIER AND STRONGER THAN THE STORM AND MAKE HIM YOUR FRIEND.

Jesus brings together a beautiful combination of both infinite power and infinite goodness. Today many people speak of power imbalances. These power imbalances often precede injustice and pain. The problem isn't a power imbalance. The problem is how the power is used. Parents have power over their children, but good parents use that power to protect and provide for their families.

Bullies misuse their power to intimidate and unjustly take from those who cannot stand against them. When fear intimidates your life with a power imbalance that seems to overwhelm your life, you must find someone stronger than the bully. Jesus is stronger than any bully.

Jesus is not only powerful, but he is *for you.* He is powerful *and* good. Power is only bad if it's misused. Jesus always uses his power for the greatest good of the universe.

We can watch in fear as financial worries, crime, pandemics, and wars threaten the security of home and family. Anxiety barges into our lives and creates havoc in our minds and bodies. During those moments, I must look to a power greater than these to bring the balance back into my favor. When the storm rages in your life, you must find someone greater than the storm. Only Jesus is greater than any storm.

YOUR DECISION

Have you placed your life in the hands of Jesus? Jesus gave some great advice about fear. He said to wisely choose your scary. The tax collector Matthew, a person whom Jesus called to be a disciple even though others viewed him as the worst of sinners, shared what Jesus said about fear,

So do not be afraid of them, for there is nothing concealed that will not be disclosed or hidden that will not be made known. What I tell you in the dark, speak in the daylight; what is whispered in your ear, proclaim from the roofs. Do not be afraid of those who kill the body but cannot kill the soul. Rather, be afraid of the

One who can destroy both soul and body in hell. Are not two sparrows sold for a penny? Yet not one of them will fall to the ground outside your Father's care. And even the very hairs of your head are all numbered. So don't be afraid; you are worth more than many sparrows. (Matthew 10:26-31)

Loss or pain have power to create fear in our lives. Jesus tells us that when you worship the God of the universe, you have no need to fear those who can only temporarily deprive you of important things or cause pain in your life. *He tells us that the greatest loss we could ever experience is separation from the God who made us, not temporary pain from the bullies around us.*

Our greatest problem is not fear and anxiety. Our greatest problem is that a holy God created us for a relationship, and we have all violated his moral law and broken that relationship. He created us for a purpose, to know him and to bear his image. We have all broken that moral law. Every one of us has lied, lusted, stolen, dishonored our parents, worshiped other gods, and used the Lord's name as a curse word.

Death is a limiter on evil. The Bible tells us the wages of sin is death. Death means a separation; your body will separate from your soul one day. And spiritual death means we will be separated from God forever in hell as Jesus mentions. Jesus says the smart person fears *that.* Some are afraid to give their lives to Christ because of what it will cost them. People may ridicule them. Jesus said if you gain the whole world and lose your soul forever, you made a bad trade. Only Jesus can bring the balance of power back in your favor.

All of us owe an infinite debt because we have sinned against an infinite God. Only the infinite Son, Jesus, could pay the ultimate price so that our inestimable debt could be forgiven. *Our only hope is that the infinite wisdom of God made a way for the love of God to satisfy the wrath of God so that we might become the children of God.*

OUR ONLY HOPE IS THAT THE INFINITE WISDOM OF GOD MADE A WAY FOR THE LOVE OF GOD TO SATISFY THE WRATH OF GOD SO THAT WE MIGHT BECOME THE CHILDREN OF GOD.

That's why Jesus came to earth. He put on human form so that he could take our death penalty. Have you decided to turn away from your sin and put your faith and trust in Jesus? Religion can't save you, only a relationship with Jesus can do that.

The most important decision of your life is what you will do with Jesus. Without him, you sit powerless against the real fears of the world. Invite Jesus into your boat and he will speak peace to your heart, because he has power to defeat your most powerful and persistent enemy—death and justice. **When you worship the God of heaven, the God of life, the God of healing, you don't need to fear hell, death, loss, or pain. But if you haven't turned away from sin and placed your trust in Christ,** *you should be scared.*

Dr. Edward Welch in his book, *Running Scared,* put it so well, "The odd thing is that fear and anxiety are running away from something, but they don't know what to run *to.* They know danger, but they don't know where to find peace and rest. If fear slows down for a minute, it realizes that peace and rest can only reside in *someone* rather than some-*thing.* A fearful child wants to sleep with her parents. On a walk through the dark woods, our fears ebb in the presence of a companion—in a pinch we will even settle for a small dog. Over the short run, anything alive will do, but we prefer an actual person who is big and strong."[10]

If fear is a personal matter, we must set out to know a person. Jesus is that person. If you give your life to the right God, fear won't be absent from your life, but it will have no power to control your life. Love God more than you fear pain. Trust God more than you fear loss. Pray to God who can bring peace to your heart. We worship a God who can redeem all loss and heal all pain. Jesus restores the balance of power in our favor. Fear him and we need not fear anything else.

---

10. Edward T. Welch, *Running Scared: Fear, Worry, and the God of Rest* (Greensboro, NC: New Growth Press, 2007), 63.

Question:

Have you surrendered your life to Jesus?

☐ YES

☐ NO

CHAPTER THREE
Scared to Death

Funerals. I don't know many people who like funerals. As a pastor, I have attended more than my share. I have watched as people have mourned silently and wailed violently. We fear death for several reasons.

I walked into a bedroom where cancer was destroying the life of one of my heroes. It's hard to know what to say in those moments. I let out an awkward, "How are you doing?" He replied, "Well, I'm not sure, I've never died before." Woody Allen famously said, "I am not afraid of death, I just don't want to be there when it happens." The process of death can be scary. We fear things that have the power to bring us pain. Death definitely qualifies for that.

We also fear those things that cause loss in our lives. Death brings loss of opportunity, relationships, and life. You will often hear those who have lost children say something like, "I will never get to see them grow up." "I will never get to walk her down the aisle." Death brings a *finality* to loss. The weeping at a funeral arises from the finality of death. There is a forever quality to the idea of passing away.

Of the many things to fear, death dominates them all. So, if you can conquer the fear of death, you can conquer all other fears. In fact, how you handle the death problem is the key to handling *all other fears.*

LIVING WITH A PRICE ON YOUR HEAD

Lazarus was a friend of Jesus. He contracted a deadly ailment and became gravely ill. Jesus received word of his sickness, but he delayed his visit until Lazarus had died and was in the tomb four days. Upon arriving near his friend's home, Martha, Lazarus' sister greeted Jesus with sorrow and pain. "If you had been here my brother would not have died."

Jesus tries to comfort his friends, but he finds himself crying at the gravesite. The shortest verse in the Bible is "Jesus wept." God cries at death. It is not his plan for mankind. Sin brought death into the world; Jesus came to bring back our opportunity at life.

People warned Jesus as he walked up to the tomb, "He's been dead four days, he's going to stink something fierce!" Jesus had them roll away the stone and he called out with a loud voice, "Lazarus, come forth!" (Someone said that the reason Jesus specifically said, "*Lazarus,* come forth," is because if he didn't, *everyone* would have come forth!) Lazarus hobbled out of the grave wrapped up like a mummy. They freed him and everyone marveled at this incredible miracle.

A while later John records one little sentence in the account of Lazarus that has profound implications to help us live courageously. This miracle caused the religious and civil leaders to want to kill Jesus. Too many people began following him and this made them jealous and afraid of losing their power.

Jesus took a break from his public ministry to avoid those who would try to kill him before the appointed time of his crucifixion.[11] Six days before Passover, Jesus showed up at Lazarus' house again and word got out that he had surfaced. While Jesus was having dinner with his friends, his enemies began to plot a way to kill him. John recounts the event,

> Meanwhile a large crowd of Jews found out that Jesus was there and came, not only because of him but also to see Lazarus, whom he had raised from the dead. So the chief priests made plans to kill Lazarus as well, for on account of him many of the Jews were going over to Jesus and believing in him. (John 12:9-11)

Notice that Jesus wasn't the only one they wanted to kill. They wanted to kill Lazarus as well! They wanted to stop Lazarus from sharing his testimony. I know I would love to sit down to listen to his story! What was their strategy? They plotted to kill him.

Now imagine this scenario. "Lazarus, if you don't stop telling people about Jesus, we are going to kill you!" Lazarus spits out

---

11. The Bible unfolds a story of God redeeming sinful man. The infinite God became human so he could die to pay our infinite debt. This was predicted by many prophets so John points out there was an "appointed time" for this event.

his drink laughing, "Been there, done that! I even have this t-shirt!" What can you do to intimidate someone that has made peace with death? "Lazarus, if you don't stop telling people about Jesus, we will torture you!" Lazarus chuckles, "Nothing you can do to me on this earth can compare to the glory that awaits me on the other side."

Because Lazarus had the advantage of seeing beyond the grave, his uncertainty and fear were eliminated. How you answer the death question will lay the foundation for how you handle all other fears.

How do you answer the death question without dying? Easy, listen to one who was dead for three days and came back to life. Instant street cred in my book. Jesus is unique in the history of mankind in that prophets predicted his life hundreds of times and hundreds of years before he lived. The prophets throughout the Old Testament predicted his birth, how he lived, and how he died. The prophecies included exquisite detail that could not have been faked. Jesus lived a perfect life. He asked those who tried to kill him,

> But because I speak the truth, you do not believe Me! Which of you can prove Me guilty of sin? If I speak the truth, why do you not believe Me? Whoever belongs to God hears the words of God. The reason you do not hear is that you do not belong to God. (John 8:45-47)

Jesus demonstrated power over nature by walking on water, commanding the wind and waves, calling fish to dive into nets, and healing people of all manner of maladies. He predicted his

31

death and resurrection, and history records these details. Jesus sets himself apart from every other religious leader (or any other kind of leader) in the history of the world.

How can we be so sure that Jesus *actually* rose from the dead? Most scholars agree on what are called, "the minimal facts" regarding the resurrection of Jesus.[12]

Some of these facts are an embarrassing testimony, the empty tomb, the appearances of Jesus post-resurrection, and skeptical and antagonistic conversions giving rise to the Christian church. Let's briefly look at each one.

Scholars look to certain criteria to discern the authenticity of historical works. One of the criteria is "embarrassing testimony." We know from common human experience that we tend to shade the truth to make ourselves look better. We rarely if ever, lie to make ourselves look *worse*. The gospel writers include accounts that make themselves look bad.

For instance, each writer includes the women who followed Jesus and stayed with him through the crucifixion. The big, strong, men (all but John), fled in fear. The women also were the first to report the empty tomb. Women's testimony was suspect during that time so if you wanted to make up a story, you wouldn't have the women testify.

---

12. For more on this go to www.garyhabermas.com. Gary Habermas has spent his life's work and literally written thousands of pages on the historical fact of the resurrection.

It was a sympathetic Pharisee, (a member of the same group of people who had Jesus crucified), who helped take Jesus' body from the cross. His disciples were nowhere to be found.

Peter betrayed his Lord! Peter, (the founder of the New Testament church), was called Satan by Jesus. If I'm Peter, I'm asking Mark to leave those things out! Why the embarrassing details if they didn't really happen? They did happen. The gospel accounts are trustworthy and the fact that they include embarrassing testimony points to these truths.

The second detail that we must account for is the empty tomb. There are only two naturalistic explanations: the friends of Jesus took the body, or the enemies of Jesus took the body. Let's examine the first option that Jesus' disciples perpetrated the greatest conspiracy of all time by taking the body and telling people Jesus rose from the dead.

There are a couple of insurmountable problems with this idea. First, it is looking at the resurrection through modern "Christian" eyes instead of the perspective of a first-century Jew. The Jews had no concept of a Messiah that would be defeated and crucified, then later rise from the dead. The Jews thought the resurrection was a general event that would take place at the end of the world with no connection to the Messiah. All the disciples were born and raised in a Jewish context. They wouldn't have the background to even fabricate such an idea.

Second, the disciples paid a heavy price for their proclamation of an empty tomb. Peter, James, and Paul were all martyred for their faith. People don't die for what they know is a lie unless they are mentally deranged. Not one disciple under pain of torture shared their deception. Not one as they faced death said, "Okay, Okay! I know where the body is!" Human nature is not one to keep secrets. How many "tell-all" books fill shelves in our homes? Two people can keep a secret if one is dead. The disciples did not steal the body and then lie about it.

What about the enemies of this new Christian movement? Did they take the body? Unlikely. What motivation would they have? They wanted to stop the early Christians from proclaiming the resurrection. All they needed to do was to produce the body. The fact that they didn't, points to an empty tomb. Neither the friends nor enemies of Jesus had the body. The tomb was empty. Jesus had conquered sin and death.

How are the appearances of a post-resurrected Jesus best explained? The vast majority of scholars acknowledge that Paul wrote First Corinthians early after the resurrection. Paul recounts the repeated appearances of the post-resurrected Jesus in an early Christian creed:

> For what I received I passed on to you as of first importance: that Christ died for our sins according to the Scriptures, that he was buried, that he was raised on the third day according to the Scriptures, and that he appeared to Cephas, and then to the Twelve. After that, he appeared to more than five hundred of the brothers and sisters at the same time, most of whom are still living, though some have fallen asleep. Then he appeared to James, then to all the apostles, and last of all he appeared

to me also, as to one abnormally born. (I Corinthians 15:3-8)

Paul states that Jesus appeared to many people after he rose from the dead. Some would say that these people were predisposed to seeing Jesus alive again and they hallucinated. Wrong. The women went to the tomb to anoint a corpse, not hail a risen Savior. The disciples were not predisposed to see Jesus alive again. They hid and grieved; they did not wait in anticipation.

Further, people don't hallucinate in unison. Just like people don't dream the same every night. Paul boldly states that many people who witnessed Jesus alive were still around to tell of it. He wrote this during the lifetime of those who had witnessed the events. If he was making it all up, no one would give Paul the time of day. They would have refuted it outright. His books would lay upon the dustbin of history like so many tabloids. Yet his historical and inspirational books are among the most read in the history of the world.

Lastly, we must explain the radical conversions of skeptics and enemies of early Christianity who led to the rise of Christianity. Paul would be case number one. Born a Jew, he was educated as a Pharisee and persecutor of the early Christians. What caused him to convert to Christianity and write half of the New Testament? He tells us in First Corinthians, "last of all he appeared to me also, as to one abnormally born" (I Corinthians

15:8). Only one thing would explain how Paul, a hostile Jew, would become a fervent Christian. Jesus had a literal "Come to Jesus" meeting with Paul and he bent the knee to his new Savior. Smartest thing anyone could ever do.

James, the brother of Jesus, struggled with his faith. In fact, he lived most of his life as a skeptic. What would it take for you to believe your older brother was God? He may *think* he's God, but do *you* think he's God? Mark records that Jesus' family thought he was crazy (Mark 3:21). John writes that "even his own brothers did not believe in him" (John 7:3).

At the cross, moments before his death, Jesus looked at his mother Mary and his disciple John and said, "Woman, behold your son!" Then He said to the disciple, "Behold your mother!" And from that hour that disciple took her to his own home" (John 19:26-27). Why would Jesus tell John that Mary was his mother? She wasn't *actually* his mother. In that culture, the eldest son would take care of a widowed mother. Jesus was the oldest and Joseph had presumably died. If the oldest brother died, the next in line would become the caretaker. James, his brother should have taken care of Mary—but he wasn't there. James was skeptical yet later he became the pastor of the church in Jerusalem.

What accounts for the conversion of skeptical James? Paul tells us it was the appearance of Jesus. "Then he appeared to James." Wouldn't you love to eavesdrop on that conversation? "Bro, it's true, I am the Messiah!"

JESUS, THE CONQUEROR

Jesus conquered our scariest enemies—sin and death. They separate us from a holy God. God poured his wrath upon Jesus who took our death penalty. Now he offers us life in the face of death. He proclaimed, "I am the resurrection and the life, he who believes in me will live, even though he dies" (John 11:25).

The life, death, and resurrection of Jesus substantiates what he says about living a courageous and meaningful life. Only he has the power to deliver us from our most powerful enemies. When you place your life into the hands of the one who conquered death, you need not let any lesser fear bully you.

THE LIFE, DEATH, AND RESURRECTION OF JESUS SUBSTANTIATES WHAT HE SAYS ABOUT LIVING A COURAGEOUS AND MEANINGFUL LIFE. ONLY HE HAS THE POWER TO DELIVER US FROM OUR MOST POWERFUL ENEMIES.

CHAPTER FOUR
Identity Thief

The things we fear speak loudly to our hearts. They demand we live according to their dictates. They subsume us into their view of who they think we should be. "You're a loser." "You're worthless." "No one likes you." "You're not going to be OK." "You could lose it all." "What will people think when they find out?" "You will be embarrassed." "They will laugh at you."

Jesus said, "You shall know the truth and the truth will set you free" (John 8:32). Therefore, knowing and understanding your true identity is a powerful foundation from which to live a courageous life.

A generation ago, the scary movies centered around personal well-being. A deranged person snuck in your house with the intent to do you harm. Then, we needed more scare. It's not just about personal harm, but enemies (Nazi's, Commies, or the enemy du jour) that threaten the entire nation. Next, the aliens came to wipe out the entire planet! Where to go but threaten the entire universe! (Think, *Avengers End Game.*) When this generation wants to feel scared, the movie writers make them feel alone and directionless. Life is scary when you don't know who you are and where you're going.

Kylo Ren, the antagonist in the last round of the Star Wars sagas, tries to intimidate Rey (the heroine) into joining him on the dark side. "We can rule together and bring a new order to the galaxy!" She resists him and he plays the most powerful card he has. He appeals to her desire to know her roots, her parents, and where she fits into the big story. Ren pressures her, "Do you want to know the truth about your parents, or have you always known? You've just hidden it away. You know the truth. Say it."

Rey begins to tear up, and under pressure she parrots, "They were nobody."

Ren pounces on this, "They were filthy junk traders, who sold you off for drinking money. They're dead in a pauper's grave in the Jakku desert. *You have no place in this story; You come from nothing. You're nothing . . . but not to me.* Join me."

What I find intriguing is when the screenwriters wanted to speak fear into this generation, when they wanted them to be anxious, when they wanted them to feel hopeless, they didn't do it with a Freddy Krueger slasher plot. They did it by removing their place, their purpose, their history, and their connection to someone who cared about them.

Fear will often appeal to your sense of identity and belonging to get you to conform to its ways. If you are to live the courageous life God designed for you, learning beyond a shadow of a doubt who you are and why you matter must become your top priority.

FEAR WILL OFTEN APPEAL TO YOUR SENSE OF IDENTITY AND BELONGING TO GET YOU TO CONFORM TO ITS WAYS.

WHO ARE YOU?
A SPECIAL CREATION OF GOD

The creator of an object determines the identity of an object. We intuitively know what a *Chevrolet* is. We know what *Kleenex* is. Many will know what a *Fender* or *Gibson* is. We know *what* they are because we know *who made them.*

Who made you? Some would say nobody. Lawrence Krauss, former professor at Yale and Arizona State wrote in his book, *A Universe from Nothing,*

> The amazing thing is that every atom in your body came from a star that exploded . . . It really is the most poetic thing I know about physics: You are all stardust. You couldn't be here if stars hadn't exploded because the elements—the carbon, nitrogen, oxygen, iron, all the

things that matter for evolution—weren't created at the beginning of time. They were created in the nuclear furnaces of stars, and the only way they could get into your body is if those stars were kind enough to explode. So, forget Jesus. The stars died so that you could be here today.

That's it. Nobody created you. Stars exploded. Other popular authors echo this sentiment. Yuval Harari, author of *"Sapiens, A Brief History of Human Kind,"* writes about who you are. Notice how the story of your origin is linked to your identity and value:

According to the science of biology, people were not "created." They have evolved. And they certainly did not evolve to be "equal." The idea of equality is inextricably intertwined with the idea of creation. The Americans got the idea of equality from Christianity, which argues that every person has a divinely created soul, and that all souls are equal before God. However, if we do not believe in the Christian myths about God, creation, and souls, what does it mean that all people are "equal"? . . . Evolution is based on difference, not on equality. Every person carries a somewhat different genetic code and is exposed from birth to different environmental influences. This leads to the development of different qualities that carry with them different chances of survival. "Created equal" should therefore be translated into "evolved differently." Just as people were never created, neither, according to the science of biology, is there a "Creator" who "endows" them with anything. There is only a blind evolutionary process, devoid of any purpose, leading to the birth of individuals. "Endowed by their creator" should be translated simply into "born."

Invigorating, isn't it? You really don't have any intrinsic value or rights; evolution has created you out of genetic material. Therefore, you are only the sum of your material parts. Biochemists sum up the chemistry of life with this acronym: CHNOPS—carbon, hydrogen, nitrogen, oxygen, phosphorus, and sulfur. That's it. That's what you are. If we could boil you down to your base chemical elements, we could get maybe twenty dollars for the chemicals. That's your value.

One more quote to drive home the point. Steven Weinberg, a professor at the University of Texas, writes in his book, *Facing Up:*

> We find that the earth on which we live is a speck of matter revolving around a commonplace star, one of billions in a galaxy of stars, which itself is only one of trillions of galaxies. Even more chilling, we ourselves are the end result of a vast sequence of breedings and eatings, the same process that has also produced the clam and the cactus . . . The human race has had to grow up a good deal in the last five hundred years to confront the fact that we just don't count for much in the grand scheme of things, and the teaching of science as a liberal art helps each of us grow up as an individual.

That's it. Clam, Cactus, Carl. Same-same. You're just going to have to deal with the fact that you don't count for much. Now go get 'em!

THE BANKRUPTCY OF EVOLUTIONARY THEORY

While Charles Darwin's theory has had a tremendous impact upon the history of science, philosophy, and religion, science has uncovered some serious flaws in the last 150 years. Many in their science departments hold on tight to the theory out of desperation for funding, stubbornness, and peer pressure. Thousands of scientists have left the theory behind looking for better evidence. You can see some of those Ph.D. level scientists catalogued on a website called DissentfromDarwin.org.

In November of 2016, a group of distinguished scientists gathered in London for a meeting of the "Royal Society of London for Improving Natural Knowledge." This is a group of prestigious scientists that dates to 1660. Its founders included the great chemist Robert Boyle, and it was later headed for twenty-four years (1703-1727), by Sir Isaac Newton—a fact that is hard to forget with Newton's death mask on prominent display in a glass case. Portraits of Boyle and Newton look down from the walls above.

The Royal Society is the world's oldest and most prestigious scientific organization. The meeting was called by a group of evolutionary biologists who have dubbed themselves "the third way." They organized the meeting because of a growing widespread dissatisfaction of the old theory of evolution. They dubbed the conference, "New Trends in Evolutionary Biology: Biological, Philosophical and Social Science Perspectives."

The meeting highlighted the gap between what the textbooks print about evolution and what is said in the peer reviewed scientific literature. Scientists are realizing that the mechanisms of mutation and natural selection lack the power to create new forms of life. So, they are looking for new theories to explain new body plans or the arrival of organ systems.

While this book is not a book on evolution, I want to highlight what scientists are learning that causes them to look elsewhere for a theory of our origins. I also recognize that some think that God could have used Darwinian evolution to achieve his ends. But God uses things that actually work. Scientists increasingly find evolution only works within strict fixed limits—at the level of microbes or within taxonomic families (i.e., dogs and cats). Let's look at some of their findings.

NO ACCOUNT FOR THE EVOLUTION OF THE MIND

How could something that lacks a mind and reasoning know the path to creating sound thinking and minds? This question troubled Darwin himself. He wondered how he could trust his own thinking if a mindless, non-thinking process built his mind. Writing to a friend, he says,

> With me, the horrid doubt always arises whether the convictions of man's mind, which has been developed from the mind of the lower animals, are of any value or at all trustworthy. Would anyone trust the convictions of a monkey's mind, if there are any convictions in such a mind?[13]

---

13. Letter to William Graham, July 3, 1881, *The Life and Letters of Charles Darwin Including an Autobiographical Chapter,* ed. Francis Darwin, (London: John Murray). Albemarle Street, 1887, 1:315-16. Cited in Alvin Plantinga, *Warrant and Proper Function,* (New York: Oxford University Press, 1993), 219.

Physical systems are governed by physical laws. Yet with our minds, we are capable of controlling physical bodies. When you raise your hand, your mind—a non-physical part of you—tells your hand—a physical part of you—what to do. Our minds can take precedence over physical laws and systems and are therefore over and above the physical.

That which is constrained by physical laws (evolution) cannot give rise to something that supersedes the physical. Therefore, man did not evolve from the physical. Here are some questions that are moving scientists away from the traditional theory of evolution:

IF our minds are the product of a random and mindless process . . .
• Then how do we know our thoughts are not random?
• How do we know we can know anything?
• How do we know our mind and senses inform us about reality?
• Have we ever seen intelligence come from randomness? A mind from a mindless process?

IF our minds are the product of a Designer's Mind . . .
• Then we can trust our thoughts to be more than random.
• We trust that we can know things.
• We can trust that our mind and senses inform us about reality.
• Have we ever seen intelligence come from intelligence? Yes, computers for example.

For more on this specific argument, see my essay entitled, *The Thinking Atheist—an Oxymoron.*[14]

THE ORIGIN OF INFORMATION

Darwin had no idea that each kind of life molecule—nucleic acids, proteins, carbohydrates, and lipids— carried vast amounts of specified information. The human DNA carries about ten thousand books worth of information, each two hundred pages in length. If you happened along the beach and saw the words, "I love Sally" scrolled in the sand with a heart shape around it would you conclude that the wind and the waves and natural processes formed it? Of course not. So, if you happened upon ten thousand books in the woods would you think they just evolved? No. Scientists are finding that the information in each living cell is far too complex for any natural process to create.

Information scientists tell us that there are five levels of information. Nature can produce the lowest levels. The first level is *statistics.* These are random generated sequences. Like monkeys at a keyboard typing: "jkii wj998ijpwuJehjeqo." While complex, this information is simply statistical. We find no message in it. Nature can produce statistics. The second level we

---

14. Carey Waldie, The Thinking Atheist, 7.19.2022,
http://www.careywaldie.com/the-thinking-atheist-an-oxymoron/

call *cosyntics.* Cosyntics are words but no message like: "grand the eats." Nature can produce content at this level as well. We see beautiful patterns in snowflakes, seashores, and crystals at this level of information. However, we find that only properly working minds can produce the higher levels of information.

The third level is *semantics;* these are words in proper linkage: "Grandpa is eating." The fourth level is *pragmatics;* this is information that requests an action: "Let's eat, Grandpa!" At the highest level we find *apobetics;* this is information that requests and anticipates a response: "Are you ready to eat, Grandpa?" Life's molecules carry the highest level of information. DNA requests responses from proteins and so much more throughout the cell. There is only one known source in the entire universe for this level of information: a mind. And the mind that designed your DNA is the most brilliant, powerful, loving, and kind Creator you will ever know.

One way to know the difference between each level of communication is to test how tolerant each level of information is to change. If we took the invitation, "Let's eat, Grandpa!" and removed just the comma, it changes the meaning completely. We go from an exciting invitation to sup with our elder to supping *on* our elder. This low tolerance for change is present in high levels of communication.

Living things carry the highest level of information. They cannot tolerate much change. We call these changes mutations. Our cells have amazing, self-correcting mechanisms precisely because they don't tolerate change very well. This leads us to the next fatal flaw Darwin knew nothing about.

MUTATIONS DO NOT PRODUCE ENOUGH POSITIVE CHANGE

The supposed engine of evolutionary change is the mutation. A mutation is a mistake in copying the DNA code from one cell to another. Even though the cell has tremendous capacity for accuracy and even correction, mistakes still happen. The problem for evolution is that mistakes do not build new kinds of organ systems or new kinds of organisms.

There are two glaring problems with mutations: first, mistakes move the organism *away* from viability not toward greater fitness, and second, there is no mechanism that creates new, novel information to code for new structures.

Dr. Geoffrey Simmons wrote in his very readable book, *What Darwin Didn't Know*, "Nearly all accidents (mutations) in nature are either silent and useless, extremely challenging, outright deforming, or simply incompatible with life. They are not capable of creating complex individuals who can paint beautiful pictures, write wonderful stories, repair cleft palates, debate political issues, or build race cars."[15]

DNA is analogous to a computer software code. If you start randomly changing the 0's and 1's, are you more likely to get a better operating system or a worse one? What if you randomly changed them for one minute? What if I gave you more time? What if you randomly changed them for a year? Ten years? Better or worse? Time is not the hero of the plot. When the mechanism is faulty, giving it more time makes it worse, not better.

Protein structures are extremely sensitive to change. For instance, there are 348 amino acids in the light-sensitive molecule rhodopsin in the human eye. People who suffer from congenital stationary night blindness, have mutations at only four different amino acid positions. When a C and A replace each other in the DNA sequence in chromosome three, (which codes for rhodopsin), it changes the amino acid from a proline to a histidine. This causes some forms of blindness from retinitis pigmentosa. Mutations break things, they don't build things.

Second, any mutational change that has the power to change the organism must take place early in the embryonic development, but those early mutations most often result in deformities or mortalities. They call it "embryonic lethal."

---

15. Geoffrey Simmons, M.D., *What Darwin Didn't Know,* (Eugene, OR: Harvest House, 2004), 30.

Think of an automobile assembly line. Early in the assembly the big structures of the frame and engine are set. This helps determine what kind of vehicle it will be. Later, paint color can be adjusted. If you set out to build a truck, it must be decided early. The color of the truck can come at the end. Research on fruit flies (illustrated in most biology textbooks), shows that late mutations (occurring late in embryonic development), are too weak to make the macro changes (like the frame of the truck) needed for macro evolution. Early mutations cause macro changes, but they often destroy the organism or create something that is so deformed it has no ability to compete in the real world—like creating a truck with only one tire.

In his ground-breaking book, *Darwin's Doubt,* Stephen Meyer writes an entire section covering seven chapters regarding this and other problems with the mechanisms of evolution. He writes,

> At the same time, mutagenesis experiments—on fruit flies as well as on other organisms such as nematodes (roundworms), mice, frogs, and sea urchins—have raised troubling questions about the role of mutations in the origin of animal body plans. If mutating the genes that regulate body-plan construction destroy animal forms as they develop from an embryonic state, then how do mutations and selection build animal body plans in the first place?[16]

---

16. Stephen C. Meyer, *Darwin's Doubt,* (HarperOne, 2013), Kindle, 257.

Lastly, the latest research has shown that even perceived beneficial mutations are created by *destroying* genetic capability not *enhancing* it.

Evolutionary expert and author of three best-selling books on the topic, Michael Behe, shares in his book, *Darwin Devolves,*

> With surpassing irony, it turns out that, as with the polar bear, Darwinian evolution proceeds mainly by damaging or breaking genes, which, counterintuitively, sometimes helps survival. In other words, the mechanism is powerfully devolutionary. It promotes the rapid loss of genetic information. Laboratory experiments, field research, and theoretical studies all forcefully indicate that, as a result, random mutation and natural selection make evolution self-limiting. That is, the very same factors that promote diversity at the simplest levels of biology actively prevent it at more complex ones. Darwin's mechanism works chiefly by squandering genetic information for short-term gain.[17]

God declares you "fearfully and wonderfully made." You are more than chemistry plus natural laws. God designed you for a purpose and you walk the planet because he placed you here. His love for you is beyond measure. You do have a place in the story! You do matter! He created you to bear his image to the watching world.[18]

---

17. Michael J. Behe, *Darwin Devolves,* (HarperOne, 2019), Kindle, 37-38.
18. We could not cover the vast research documented regarding the failings of Darwinian theory here. I would recommend the following resources for further study: *Signature in the Cell* and *Darwin's Doubt* by Stephen C. Meyer; *Undeniable* by Doug Axe; *Darwin Devolves* by Michael J. Behe; and *What Darwin Didn't Know* by Geoffrey Simmons.

GOD DECLARES YOU "FEARFULLY
AND WONDERFULLY MADE." YOU
ARE MORE THAN CHEMISTRY PLUS
NATURAL LAWS.

CHAPTER FIVE

Significant You

I was rushed into emergency surgery to repair a burst appendix that was now four days old (I delayed going to the doctor). I had never been unconscious in my life. I had never been drunk, high, or under the influence of a foreign substance. As I came to in the recovery room, I rested in a semi-conscious state. As soon as they could, the nurses began to move me into my room for the next few days.

While they wheeled me down the hall, I suddenly realized I had no pants! Like a bad dream in high school, I was now in public without my pants! Of course, I was covered up by blankets, but in my drug-induced state, panic set into my heart. I began to yell through the halls of the hospital, "Who stole my pants! Who stole my pants!" The nurses re-introduced my family to me, and I responded, "Are these the people who stole my pants?!" The world can be a scary place when you don't know who you are or who stole your pants!

Remember: *Fear will often appeal to your sense of identity and belonging to get you to conform to its ways.* If you are to live the courageous life God designed for you, you must embed in your heart beyond a shadow of a doubt **who you are** and **why you matter.**

When a child works hard on a piece of art, they proudly bring it to you. You take it into your hands and rotate it in various directions trying to answer one question: "What *is* it?" Of course, you don't want to communicate that the art is so bad you cannot discern what the child created. So, it's better to say, "Tell me about this!"

From encounters like these, we learn three important truths about identity. First, identity comes from the creator, in this case, the child prodigy. Second, the creator/owner of an object sets the value of the object. Third, when we know what an object is, we know how best to use it. Purpose flows out of essence, and essence flows from the creator.

ESSENCE: WHAT YOU CAN'T STOP BEING

Essence means "the core of what we are." So, your identity cannot be changed. It is what you cannot stop being. What we cannot stop being, is a special creation of the living God made in his image. I will say it again for emphasis, *you are a special creation, made in the image of God.* The first thing that should come to our mind whenever the question arises, "What am I?" is "I am a special creation made in the image of God." You hold a unique place in the universe, and nobody can take that away from you.

What does that mean? There are some things about us that are like some things about God. Why did God create you in his image? In ancient times an emperor would command artisans to create statues of himself to be placed in remote parts of his empire. These symbols would declare that the emperor ruled here. So, God placed humanity as living symbols of himself on earth to represent his reign. Our role is to co-rule with God over his creation. We were created to help run the family business of the Trinity, to reign over all that God has made. Our task is to make our world, more like heaven. Humans are to be God's visible representatives, ruling creation as God would rule it.

WE WERE CREATED TO RUN THE FAMILY BUSINESS OF THE TRINITY, TO REIGN OVER ALL THAT GOD HAS MADE.

Other facets of the "imago Dei" include the power of our reason, language, moral awareness, self-consciousness, freedom of choice, imagination, immortality, and the power of creativity.

55

Psalm 8 tells us of our unique place in the universe:

1 O LORD, our Lord, your majestic name fills the earth!
Your glory is higher than the heavens.
2 You have taught children and infants
to tell of your strength,
silencing your enemies
and all who oppose you.
3 When I look at the night sky and see the work of your
fingers—the moon and the stars you set in place—
4 what are mere mortals that you should think about them,
human beings that you should care for them?
5 Yet you made them only a little lower than God
and crowned them with glory and honor.
6 You gave them charge of everything you made,
putting all things under their authority—
7 the flocks and the herds
and all the wild animals,
8 the birds in the sky, the fish in the sea,
and everything that swims the ocean currents.
9 O LORD, our Lord, your majestic name fills the earth!

ONLY THE OWNER HAS POWER TO DETERMINE VALUE

From time to time, I try to buy wedding rings from audience members. I ask if I can look at them. Surprisingly, they remove it from their finger and hand it to me. I look at it and assess its value. I then will say, "Wow, this is a beautiful ring, I will give you ten dollars for it." How do you think they respond? They scoff at that offer. I then proceed to up my offer. "One hundred? Five hundred? One thousand?" Once I get to around five thousand dollars, I have the husband's attention. Depending on the sentimental value the wife has for the ring, I may have caused some division in the home.

Who determines the value of the ring? The owner. I can only offer a price; I cannot *tell* her what it's worth.

Who owns you? Whoever owns you, sets your value. The question of ownership is one of the most important questions you will have to answer. Some claim, "I own myself." Really? By what logic? Are you responsible for you being here? Did you decide one day you wanted to walk planet earth and then you picked a couple of human parents to conceive you? Nope.

God owns you by virtue of his creation of you *and* his purchasing of you. The owner of anything always determines the value and the owner determines the value by accepting an offer for purchase. What is the owner willing to take in exchange for it? How much is someone willing to pay for it? What did God pay for you? That is your price tag. God paid Jesus for you.

Mark 10:45 tells us, "For even the Son of Man did not come to be served, but to serve, and to give his life as a ransom for many." John 3:16 says, "For God so loved the world that he gave his one and only Son, that whoever believes in him shall not perish but have eternal life." God so loved *you!* God created you and adopted you. What did he pay for you? The life of his Son. You have a Jesus price tag. How much is Jesus, the eternal Son of God worth? He is priceless, yet that is what it cost God to purchase us from the sin-debt we owed. You, therefore, are priceless as well. You cost Jesus to God. Who can change what God has done for you?

No parent with demeaning words, no teacher, or coach, or brother, or sister, or co-worker, or pastor can take one cent of value from you. You may have had people in your past proclaim that you have little value. By their actions they may have implied that you have little value. None of that could be further from the truth. They simply didn't *recognize your value.* You are a priceless child of God—created and purchased by God himself.

WE ARE ALL LOOKING FOR A PLACE AND A FACE

As a pastor, I get the privilege of hearing the life stories of many great people. They often find me when their lives are not going well. We are products of the many choices we make during our lives. **We have the power to choose, but once the choice is made, it has power over us.** So many of these stories start well and then take a turn. The downhills usually start with this phrase, "Then I began hanging out with the wrong crowd."

Their peer group began to pressure them to make unhealthy choices. They knew these choices had negative consequences, but they chose them anyway. What drives people to make poor choices? Fear. Fear of loss. Fear of not being accepted. Fear of being alone. Fear of ridicule. Fear of not being loved. *We all want a place to belong and a face to confer value upon us.* Marketers know these desires drive our decisions—especially when they sell products that must get past natural barriers in our lives.

When I sit around a campfire and smoke begins to blow into my face, I take evasive measures. I lean away from it. I stand and turn my back and eventually move. Inhaling deeply of the smoke is the *last* thing I would naturally do. I remember the first time I tried a cigarette. My body convulsed and violently coughed. To continue to propagate their business, tobacco companies must get past our natural tendency to reject smoke from our lungs. How do they do this? They tap into something even more primal than the desire to run from smoke—the desire to *be somebody to somebody.*

The savvy marketer will create a persona—a face that you want to identify with. The Marlboro Man and Joe Camel appeal to who we want to be. We want to be cool; we want to be accepted; we want to be fun. Wayne McLaren (one of the original Marlboro men) died of lung cancer in 1992 at age 51 after 25 years of smoking.

His modeling job with Marlboro was followed by an anti-smoking campaign that lasted until his death. "I've spent the last month of my life in an incubator and I'm telling you, it's just not worth it," McLaren told a Los Angeles Times reporter from his deathbed in Newport Beach, where he lay with several tubes connected to his body.

A week after he died, his mother Louise told The Times some of McLaren's last words were, "Take care of the children. Tobacco will kill you, and I am living proof of it." (One Marlboro Man never smoked or drank, he lived to age 88. But he inspired many people to think that the good life looks like Marlboro.)

The average age of a new smoker is between 13 and 16. Why? During adolescence, our search intensifies for a place and a face. We want a face to confer value and a place to make a difference. If we do not find our value and our place in the larger story in a legitimate, healthy way, fear will drive us to find it in an unnatural and damaging way.

If you embed deep in your soul the truth that your value is hidden in Christ, the fears that root themselves in your desire to be somebody to someone will weaken their pull upon you. Your worth is conferred to you by God. You carry essential value. *You cannot stop being valuable.*

DOING THE WORK

Making truth transformative takes work. We must take the acknowledgment of truth in the rational part of ourselves and push it into our emotional and volitional selves. As a flight instructor, I can talk you through most any maneuver without much experience on your part. You acknowledge what I am saying and perform the corresponding action. But if I stop talking, you will either freeze or panic.

My goal as a flight instructor is to have you learn the truth so well, that you act according to it regardless of stress, emotional state, or pressure. This takes work. We use all of your senses. We train you in procedures and skills. You listen to the sounds, you feel the performance of the aircraft, you see yourself in relation to the unchanging horizon and act in the best interest of yourself and passengers.

MAKING TRUTH TRANSFORMATIVE TAKES WORK. WE MUST TAKE THE ACKNOWLEGMENT OF TRUTH IN THE RATIONAL PART OF OURSELVES AND PUSH IT INTO OUR EMOTIONAL AND VOLITIONAL SELVES.

Dealing with fear is no different. We accumulate events and responses over our lifetime and develop coping mechanisms for many of them that tap into our primal desires. Someone does not affirm us, and we respond. They reject us and we respond. We incur abuse, abandonment, and pain. Our body learns a response to these events and tries to protect us. If the protective mechanisms are based on the truths of who we are in Christ and our value in God, we can move through these situations in a healthy way. But for most of us, we trained ourselves on fears which were not always based on truth.

It takes work to re-train our souls to respond to true things. In the flight instructor academy, they emphasize teaching the right way to do something the first time because what you learn first, you remember best. They call this the law of primacy. That is why childhood and adolescent experiences imprint upon us so deeply. We learn so many things for the first time. If the coping mechanisms we learned during that time created negative responses in us, we must take the time to reprogram the soul. Reprogramming our souls according to the truths of God's universe takes work. But the result is freedom.

THE FIRST TASK: LEARNING THE TRUTH OF WHO GOD IS AND WHO YOU ARE

This exercise helped transform my thinking and thousands of others. If we carry false views of God and false views of ourselves, we will remain vulnerable to illegitimate fears. Take the time to work through this study. Reject the lies about God and affirm the truth about him.

Go through and declare these truths each day when you wake up and before bed like this: "I renounce the lie that my heavenly Father is distant and disinterested and affirm that he is intimate and involved. I renounce the lie that my heavenly Father is insensitive or uncaring and affirm the truth that he is kind and compassionate." Write out the Scriptures and memorize the ones that really speak to you.

I renounce the lie that my heavenly Father is:
1. distant and disinterested
2. unwise and unable to guide me to the best life
3. insensitive, stern, or demanding
4. passive or cold
5. absent or too busy for me
6. never satisfied with what I do, impatient, or angry
7. mean, cruel, or abusive
8. trying to take all the fun out of life
9. controlling or manipulative
10. condemning or unforgiving
11. nitpicking, nagging, or perfectionistic

I accept the truth that my heavenly Father is:
1. intimate and involved (Psalm 139:1-18)
2. God who knows me and what he created me for and wants to guide me into the abundant life (John 10: 1-10, Proverbs 3:5-6)
3. kind and compassionate (Psalm 103:8-14); accepting, filled with joy, and loving (Zephaniah 3:17; Romans 15:7)
4. warm and affectionate (Isaiah 40:11; Hosea 11:3,4)
5. always with me and eager to spend time with me (Jeremiah 31:20; Ezekiel 34:11-16; Hebrews 13:5)
6. patient, slow to anger, and pleased with me in Christ (Exodus 34:6; 2 Peter 3:9)
7. loving, gentle, and protective of me (Psalm 18:2; Isaiah 42:3; Jeremiah 31:3).

8. trustworthy; wanting to give me a full life; His will is good, perfect, and acceptable for me (Lamentations 3:22, 23; John 10:10; Romans 12:1,2).

9. full of grace and mercy, and He gives me freedom to fail (Luke 15:11-16; Hebrews 4:15,16)

10. tenderhearted and forgiving; His heart and arms are always open to me (Psalm 130: 1-4; Luke 15:17-24)

11. committed to my growth and proud of me as His growing child (Romans 8:28, 29; 2 Corinthians 7:4; Hebrews 12:5-11)[19]

---

19. This exercise has been powerful in my own life. It is adapted from Neil T. Anderson's, *Leading Teens to Freedom in Christ* (Ventura, CA: Gospel Light Publications, 1997). This is a great resource for parents, youth ministers, and students.

THE FATHER'S BLESSING: PRAY THIS OVER YOURSELF EVERY DAY (MORNING AND EVENING)

In the name of Jesus Christ, I am blessed with the blessing of my heavenly Father. I am of great value in his sight, he has created me, and he has purchased me out of death and sin and placed me in the Kingdom of light. He calls me his son/daughter and I give him great pleasure (Eph. 1:5). He has forgiven my sins and given me access to his presence. He unconditionally loves me and gives my repentant heart grace and forgiveness when I disobey and fail, and grace to walk in power and victory (Heb. 4:16; I John 1:9).

I am priceless in his sight. I am a significant part of my Father's redemption plan. He has called me and given me authority as his child to represent Him. He has commissioned me and commanded me to display the love of Christ.

My heavenly Father is with me and for me. If I walk in his ways and learn his Word, he promises to give me guidance, wisdom, and correction to see that my life will make a difference and bear much fruit, for I am his child, in whom he is well pleased.

CHAPTER SIX
The Courage of Humility

People are scary. Social situations often induce anxious, fearful, and even panicked responses. When teaching new flight students, I have watched strong, successful people absolutely freeze. Not because they have taken the controls of a flying machine (although that does happen). The flying does not scare them. But there is one aspect of flying that strikes fear in the most courageous leaders: Keying the microphone to talk to air traffic control! Why do you think this is one of the frightening parts of learning to fly? People. People can be scary.

Once you key that mic, God, and everyone can hear the tremble in your voice. Seasoned airline pilots will listen to your requests. Cranky, stressed, air-traffic controllers will impatiently await your statements. They speak a language all their own. Every word is recorded and public record.[20] Your words, presentation, and inflections will instantly betray your rookie status.

These instances represent a thousand different situations where life in social or professional situations breed fear. Those

---

20, Go here to listen to Harrison Ford's conversation when he landed on a taxiway! https://www.youtube.com/watch?v=tzy9jCFkOIw&t=1s&ab_channel=VASAviation-

with and without social anxiety fear exposure to public scrutiny. Dread rises in their hearts at the thought of performing, speaking, gathering, or meeting new people. I have seen younger folks afraid of making a phone call. At the root of these fears lies the specter of humiliation or harsh judgments of others. These judgments often reinforce what others have said and the running dialogue they have in their head. "I'm dumb." "Nobody wants to be around me." "I'm a failure." Overcoming these fears will make life more enjoyable and fruitful.

INSECURITY KILLS

We all crave security. We all want to be wanted and valued. If you don't settle these questions early in your life, you will filter all your conversations and experiences through your insecurities. Then protective mechanisms will kick in and you will either fight or flee. You will fight back with your words or fists. You will become a skilled spear-thrower like King Saul (see I Samuel 8-19). His jealousy drove him to throw spears at a young David. You will grow to become jealous and a bitter backbiter.

Or you will flee. You will build walls so nobody can touch your heart. You will withdraw from risky situations and relationships. Those you can't flee from like spouses, parents, siblings, and children can make you feel trapped. And you will fight or run even more. If you can't physically flee, you will look to escape through a virtual world of fantasy or pornography. Living and caring for people can be risky.

C.S Lewis in *The Four Loves,* put it this way,

> To love is to be vulnerable. Love anything and your heart will be wrung and possibly broken. If you want to make sure of keeping it intact you must give it to no one, not even an animal. Wrap it carefully round with hobbies and little luxuries; avoid all entanglements. Lock it up safe in a casket or coffin of your selfishness. But in that casket–safe, dark, motionless, airless–it will change. It will not be broken; it will become unbreakable, impenetrable, and irredeemable. The only place you can really be free from the dangers of love is hell."

HOW TO BREAK FREE FROM INSECURITY

First, you must root your value in the untouchable truth that God created you and he purchased you. You are unique in the universe and Jesus purchased your redemption with his own life. You have a Jesus price tag. You are worth Jesus. In other words, you are of infinite value.

No person can say or do anything to truly affect your value. You must regularly affirm your value and get this truth deep into your soul. Your primary identity is that of a child of God, nobody can change that. (Keep working through the exercises from the previous chapter.)

Second, you must address negative words or actions people have spoken or done to you that have wounded or created an environment where you felt of little value. This happens to everyone. Even people who don't mean to wound you can say something that pierces your heart. If you don't deal with these, they will feed your insecurities and you will filter even more of their actions through your filter. This creates a deadly spiral of emotions and negative interpretations.

The first step to breaking free of those haunting thoughts is to identify their root and apply the power of grace to them. Ask God to bring to your mind those words and people that have wounded you, shaped your thinking, and fed insecurities.

YOU ARE UNIQUE N THE UNIVERSE AND JESUS PURCHASED YOUR REDEMPTION WITH HIS OWN LIFE. YOU HAVE A JESUS PRICE TAG. YOU ARE WORTH JESUS. IN OTHER WORDS, YOU ARE OF INFINITE VALUE.

Prayer: "I thank you for your kindness and patience with me. I know I have not always been patient and kind to others, and I thank you that you have forgiven me. I ask you to bring to my mind all the people I need to forgive. I ask you to bring to the surface any pain that they caused in my life so I can choose to forgive."

As names and instances come to your mind, write them down. Don't hold back the emotions that may come flooding into your heart. It's OK to feel hurt, betrayed, or belittled. These are normal reactions to living through such instances. You don't want to stop there, however.

Take each name and instance and bring them to the cross. The cross was placed on the town dump. When life hands us a bag of garbage, take it to the dump, don't smell it all day by letting negative, lying thoughts accuse and mock you continually.

You can use this prayer as a model. Put your own heart into it. "Lord, I forgive _____ for _____. Lord, I release all these people to You, and I release my right to seek revenge. I choose not to hold on to my bitterness and anger, and I ask You to heal my damaged emotions. And I renounce and disown any negative and lying words they have spoken over my life through word or deed. I declare I am priceless and gifted to make a difference in the world, in Jesus' name, Amen." Now destroy the list.

Moving forward, continue to merchandise in grace. Keep short accounts. People will continually offend you. (And you will offend them.) Overlook insults, assume the best about people and their motives—especially those close to you. They care about you. Negatively interpreting the actions or words of others will kill relationships. I think it's better to assume the best in others (unless they have given you good reasons to not trust them), than to continually consume yourself with the internal battle of what you think they must be thinking about you.

Remember this about forgiveness: Forgiveness is not forgetting, it's not saying what happened was right, it's not even trusting that person again. It's an act of the will; a choice, not a feeling. Let them off your hook—on to God's hook. You know you have freedom when you no longer hold a grudge, ill will, or desire for revenge. True freedom will be yours when you can pray a blessing upon them.

You may face past decisions that you regret. You must let yourself off the hook as well. Receive grace from God, so guilt and regret have no power over you. Walk in that grace and new identity of a forgiven child of God.

THINKING OF YOURSELF LESS

True humility is the key to handling social situations. Humility is not thinking less of yourself but thinking of yourself less. Knowing your value is rooted in God's love, you are free to focus on the hearts and needs of others. Anxiety demands you think of you. Fear demands you bow to its demands. Humility frees you to look to the needs of others.

Imagine your boss asks you to speak to your professional association next week. How would you feel about that? Anxious?

Public speaking routinely appears at the top of the list of fear-inducers. Usually ahead of scary things like spiders, mice, and being trapped in a small space. (Snakes usually take the top spot.) The lessons learned in preparing for a speaking engagement will help you in any social situation.

As a pastor, I have spoken publicly thousands of times, often to hostile audiences. I still get nervous. I have developed a system that will help anyone conquer these fears.

First, get to know your audience and pray yourself in love with them. When I spend time with God, he helps me love better. I must love the people more than I fear them. Love casts out fear! When I step to the front to share, I have already settled it in my heart that those before me are valuable, priceless people made in the image of God, and they deserve my best. I found I either agonize in prayer or agonize in presenting. When you genuinely love your audience, it stops becoming about you as much as it is about serving people well. When you genuinely love those in any social gathering, you can focus on them instead of your anxieties.

Second, devote time to preparation and practice. The secret to looking natural as a speaker (or many other disciplines) is working out the unnatural and awkward parts through practice. Very few people can deliver a powerful extemporaneous speech. If they can, they've talked about that subject many times before. It wasn't their first rodeo. The work behind the scenes makes the moments in front of the curtain successful.

You can prepare for any social situation. When we learn challenging maneuvers as pilots, we often use flight simulators to place us in those situations *before* we actually get there. We rehearse them until we can operate proficiently in stressful situations. We can do the same for social gatherings.

Before you speak or head to the party, visualize yourself focusing on others. Picture yourself putting people at ease, meeting, and chatting with individuals. Remember, other people feel nervous like you. Humility helps you rest internally so you can focus on others. You have no need to protect yourself so help those around you feel welcome.

Taking the initiative to break the ice shows you are interested in the person. It honors them. You are saying— "You are valuable, you are interesting, I want to get to know you." Not taking the initiative to break the ice says, "You are not valuable, you are not interesting, you are not worth my time." (You may be thinking I'm shy or I'm nervous), but what you are communicating is that my shyness, or my nervousness is more important than honoring you and helping you feel welcome.

Starting a conversation opens the door to sharing the good stuff you have and creates an opportunity for them to share the good stuff they have. One of my mentors kept a small list of opening questions that would begin thoughtful conversation. Memorize a few of these. Once you find what someone is passionate about, you're off and running.

Here's a sample of some good opening questions after you introduce yourself:

- Tell me about your family
- What do you do for work?
- Tell me your story? (My favorite)
- What do you enjoy doing in your spare time?
- What have you been reading?
- Where did you grow up?

Once you find a line of questioning that clicks, enjoy where the conversation takes you. Don't forget to SMILE! Use their name often. Open your arms and lean slightly forward. Show interest with your eyes and body language.

God will turn your pain into a platform to help those in need. As you keep short accounts and allow the powers of grace and humility to guide your relationships, you are free to serve others. And Jesus said, the greatest people are the greatest servants.

GOD WILL TURN YOUR PAIN INTO A PLATFORM TO HELP THOSE IN NEED. AS YOU KEEP SHORT ACCOUNTS AND ALLOW THE POWERS OF GRACE AND HUMILITY TO GUIDE YOUR RELATIONSHIPS, YOU ARE FREE TO SERVE OTHERS.

CHAPTER SEVEN
Failure Isn't Fatal; It's Feedback

Often our failures create a storyline in our head that taunts us. We can be our worst critics. Perfectionism can drive us to anxiety and fear. When you follow Christ with your life, he will lead you on many great adventures. He will stretch you and grow you. And there will be moments when you fail. Failure is a normal part of life. How you handle failure will determine the level of success in your life. If you have a failure of character, apologize to those you have hurt: God and others. Then make a concerted effort to grow in that area. Ask God to help you, renew your mind with the Scriptures that speak to that issue, and assess your relationships and how they influence you.

If you have a failure of performance, *assess,* then *progress.* Assess what went wrong and make the necessary adjustments ("pro" means advancing; "gress" is a degree of scale or value). If you keep doing what you're doing, you'll keep getting what you're getting. Remind yourself that your value is not in your performance but is hidden in the love God has for you.

Use failure as feedback for growth and progress. You can't get an honest assessment of your skills or character until you put them to the test. Remember, when we walk with Jesus, failure isn't fatal, you are free to take greater risks. Try new things. Too many people are afraid to try new things because they fear failure. They fear looking foolish. Be a fool for God! Take risks, learn, and grow. Use failure as feedback. Nobody has great successes without failures.

BECOMING BLUE

Each year my hometown hosts a fantastic airshow with many military aircraft and demonstration teams. My favorite is the Blue Angels. The power and speed of the F-18s they fly is unmatched by other teams. A team of filmmakers followed them for a year and documented the process to become a Blue Angel.

Upon arrival at their new training facility, the commander greets them with these words, "Your life has just changed in ways you cannot comprehend . . . you will find the debriefs and criticism you get constructive, painful, and blunt."

During the most critical phase of their training, they fly three times a day for ten weeks. Their day begins with a pre-dawn briefing. They go through each maneuver mentally using the power of visualization.

After each flight they debrief knowing that small failures aren't fatal, even at 500 miles per hour. But failure to *learn* from those failures could be fatal. Every flight maneuver is filmed from the ground and gone over with a fine-tooth comb. An essential part of the debriefing is "taking a safety." Each pilot ruthlessly self-evaluates every mistake. This process creates a tremendous bond of trust amongst the team because a teachable pilot is a humble pilot. A humble pilot is a safe pilot. After confessing their "safeties" to the team, they finish with a proclamation: "I will fix my mistakes and I am glad to be here."

The commander gives great advice, "You'll get there but only if you're patient and you can take a beating and come back the next day and say, "I'm glad to be here and I'll do a better job tomorrow." "It's hard, you're not very good at it for a long time." Persistence, failing, and learning are vital for becoming the best God created you to be.

IF YOU WANT TO BE GOOD YOU MUST BE WILLING TO BE BAD

Nobody is born excellent at anything but eating, sleeping, and eliminating. While those are important activities, nobody will pay you to do any of them. A rich and fulfilling life will require you to learn higher-level skills. When you were a child, learning things like language and movement came naturally. You were unencumbered by fear or intimidation. You learned difficult motor skills without breaking a sweat.

Something happens as we get older. We start to care what others think. We begin to compare ourselves with our peers and rank ourselves in relation to them. We start to fear failure and embarrassment. Instead of naturally learning new things, we can talk ourselves right out of new skills, adventures, and experiences. We want to go back to the days where eating and sleeping were all we were expected to do.

LIFE'S GREATEST TREASURES ARE NOT AT THE SURFACE. THEY MUST BE RELENTLESSLY PURSUED. TO ACHIEVE GREAT THINGS, YOU MUST PLOD THROUGH AN ONSLAUGHT OF FAILURE, BOREDOM, SWEAT, AND SOMETIMES TEARS.

But life's greatest treasures are not at the surface. They must be relentlessly pursued. To achieve great things, you must plod through an onslaught of failure, boredom, sweat, and sometimes tears. Far too many quit their life's goals before they achieve them simply because they were not willing to be bad before they could be good. If you want to be good, you must be willing to be bad.

Nobody is born to fly. Every flight student I have ever had, came to me with no inherent ability to aviate. As their flight instructor, I saved their lives (and mine) many times before they could pilot a plane. Those who achieved their dream of becoming a pilot persevered during the times of poor performance. It's what we call learning!

The Gracie family invented Brazilian Jiu Jitsu. The techniques in BJJ are so effective they teach the student to tap the hand repeatedly to let the instructor know when to let go of the technique. The motto is, "tap, snap or nap." (Translated: If you don't tap, your limb will snap, or you will fall unconscious.) They say, "The path to black belt is 2,000 taps." They know the secret; if you want to be good, you must be willing to be bad.

EMBRACE THE PROCESS

Learning is a process, and failure is part of that process. Here are some tips on learning well:

1. Establish a benchmark. What is your goal? Make it specific. In flight-school we called these Airman Certification Standards. They are objectives set by the Federal Aviation Administration that spell out exactly what goals need to be met to obtain your pilot's license. Early in the training, they seem so difficult and hard to accomplish. But you must be willing to be bad before you're good. Those who succeed, use the benchmarks as a focal point and measuring stick.

2.   Learn the fundamentals. What you learn first, you remember best. Don't rush ahead to try to arrive at the fun part of your discipline by neglecting the fundamentals. Don't practice bad habits or you will just reinforce poor technique. This may seem like a short-cut to competency, but it will cost you when you get to the higher levels of your discipline.

3.   Go slow and perfect. When learning complex techniques, start slow and proceed perfectly. When learning scales on an instrument, don't rush it. Sound each note with clarity and good timing. When learning an athletic move, repeat it slowly and perfectly to allow your muscles to learn the correct movement. In time, you may go faster, never compromise technique for speed. Speed will come, let it come with good form.

4.   Isolate and replicate. Your brain is an amazing thing. It can direct your body to do very different things at once. To help it put techniques together, isolate each movement. When you fly a helicopter, you must manage four controls at once. No one can do it at first. Early in training, the instructor controls three of them and the student just focuses on one. In time, the instructor gradually hands over the other controls until the student can control all four. If you're struggling to put it all together, isolate, then replicate. Just play the left hand, focus on the kick drum, do one thing slowly and perfectly, then slowly add the other skills. Your brain will work its magic in time.

5. Consistency counts. The best students practice consistently. Fifteen minutes of practice each day is better than one hour of practice every four days. Repetition is the mother of skill.

6. Visualize. There is little difference in the learning centers of your brain between you imagining the activity and doing the activity. Harness the power of your imagination. I regularly work through checklists and maneuvers in my mind before a lesson or flight test. This will work for your driver's test, a big speech, or a huge game.

7. Push through plateaus. If you learn anything, you will experience times where your performance levels off or even gets worse. These are normal! Continue to persevere, you will meet with success!

YOU ARE GOD'S GIFT TO THE WORLD. SERVE!

The power of a secure heart gives you the freedom to serve and even to make mistakes and still know you are loved and valuable. Often fear keeps us from blessing the world with our gifts and talents.

As you serve others, the light in your heart begins to shine even brighter and you realize that you can make a positive contribution to the world. And know in your heart if you toil in obscurity, far from the spotlight, or credit of men, God sees and applauds, and he will reward you publicly one day!

Just know it's OK to not be OK. We are all people in process and perfectionism will lead to anxiety but learning from our mistakes is normal growth. Let grace and humility blaze the path to competency. Competency gives birth to confidence and a confident, humble person has power to bless the world. Learn to laugh at yourself. Some things are just funny. Remember failing cannot touch your value.

Jesus made it clear that greatness never comes from demanding our own way or parading our accomplishments so we can soak in the accolades from the masses. Greatness comes from serving.

The greatest restaurants have great service. The best auto dealers have the greatest service. The finest stores have top-notch service. Our police officers and elected officials are called public servants. There is an inherent value in serving. When you join the military, we say you joined the service.

Many people wish for position. They want to showcase their gifts. Perhaps they are even better qualified to fill the position they seek than the one currently filling it. Positions aren't bad. However, you can attain them in a bad way. The Lord wants us to maintain a servant's heart, and he will bless us with positions as he sees fit.

A servant has five defining characteristics. First, servants are hard to offend. They are not thinking of themselves. They are thinking, "How can I best serve the team? What needs can I meet today?" One of the best ways to know if you're really a servant is by how you respond when you're treated like one.

Second, servants don't need to be seen, but they aren't afraid to be seen if it allows them to serve better. Some love being out front, they are natural leaders or performers. Others shudder at the thought of giving a speech. A true servant will serve anywhere that best suits the mission—out front or behind the curtain.

Third, servants don't seek status, but will accept responsibility if it enables them to serve better. For a true servant, it's never about status or titles, it's about getting the mission done and honoring people in the process. A servant doesn't expect accolades or attention. They are happy to serve. They serve as unto God. Even if their leaders don't recognize them, they know that God sees them. Work is worship to a true servant.

Fourth, servants can move freely from a high task to a lowly one if it allows them to serve better. We tend to rank our jobs. Some we place at a higher-level, some we say are low. Some are important and others not so much. But under God, every task done for his glory is of eternal significance. A true servant can perform a task viewed as "important" one minute and a "non-important" task the next.

Fifth, servants (great people) are faithful. Many want God to use them in the "big" things, but they haven't been faithful in the "little" things. The Bible likens a person who lacks faithfulness to a bad tooth or a twisted ankle (see Proverbs 25:19).

If you have a habit of letting people down with your faithlessness, don't expect to do much for God. You may have great talent and a calling on your life, but if you don't cultivate faithfulness and reliability in your life, you are a bad tooth.

Your work is of eternal significance and excellence requires commitment. If you are faithful, God will use you. God calls in stages, testing our character. Many have a calling but prove faithless in the preparation stages, so they remain mired in tasks that seem beneath them. They feel God has called them to greater things, but how faithful have they been in the small things? Are they an example of faithfulness in prayer, study, promptness, and following through tasks to completion? Don't let fear or anxiety (or anything) keep you from staying faithful to your call.

As you persevere in your gifts, talents, and failures, God will bring you to a place to reach back and help others along the journey. He will make a platform out of your pain. On this platform you can encourage the scared and strengthen the weak. I can't wait to see what God will make of your failures! Remember, people don't drown by falling in the water, they drown by staying there. Get up, try again, and soon you will be rescuing others!

In 1904, St. Louis hosted the Louisiana Purchase Exposition in conjunction with the Olympic games. Forty-two states and fifty-three nations took part in the great celebration. Among the vendors were two men, one with an ice cream booth and the other sold hot waffles. As the crowds grew, both men did tremendous business. After a few days, the waffle vendor ran out of the cardboard plates upon which he had been serving his waffles with three different kinds of topping. He went to the different vendors, but no one would sell him any plates. All the other vendors jealously guarded their supplies.

The ice cream vendor with great sympathy said to the waffle man, "That's the way the old waffle crumbles. It looks like you would be better off selling ice cream for me."

The waffle vendor considered his alternative, which was attempting to serve his waffles without plates and watching the syrup run down the sleeves of his irate customers. He agreed to buy the ice cream at a discount and resell it at his booth near the arcade.

The waffle vendor tried to recoup his losses by selling the ice cream at small profit margin. In the back of his mind, he thought about the waffle ingredients going to waste. He had spent his life savings trying to capitalize on the huge crowds this fair would bring.

Suddenly, an idea struck him like a bolt of lightning. He wondered why he hadn't thought of it before. He was sure it would work. At home the next day, the waffle vendor made a batch of one thousand waffles and pressed them thin with an iron. He then rolled them in to a circular pattern with a point at the bottom.

The next morning, he sold all his ice cream before noon and all one thousand waffles with three different toppings as well! Because of the adversity posed by the problem of running out of plates, he progressed all of civilization by inventing the ice cream cone! I can't wait to see how you will bless those around you as God makes you a courageous gift to the world!

TOP TEN FEARS:

#1 SNAKES
#2 PUBLIC SPEAKING
#3 HEIGHTS
#4 RODENTS
#5 FLYING
#6 BEING TRAPPED IN A SMALL SPACE
#7 SPIDERS AND INSECTS
#8 THUNDER AND LIGHTNING
#9 BEING ALONE AT NIGHT
#10 DOGS

CHAPTER EIGHT

Why am I So Scared?

A few years ago, I received a phone call inviting me to sit on a panel of experts discussing a very controversial issue at our local college. I agreed to represent the side of those against overturning a decades long policy that would affect the very fabric of society. I asked the organizer who else would represent our side. She gave me the name of a prominent public policy advocate who did things like this for a living.

For weeks leading up to the forum, I tried to get ahold of him to receive some small area of focus for me and let him know I was counting on him to carry the rest of the evening. I could not get him to respond to me. Finally, hours before the open forum, he answered the phone and told me that he couldn't make it. I was on my own.

"Great," I thought, "Surely there will be others there that will help to defend our position." Well, as it turned out. I entered a very large auditorium full of people clearly against my stance. I would estimate 95% of the hostile crowd came in support of the opposite team.

As I took the stage, eight other people joined me. ALL of them were against my position. It was me against eight other debaters and a hostile audience. My poor wife was in the very back row.

For an hour and a half, I felt like my soul had left my body. I talked, argued, and bantered as best I could while praying for the rapture. At the end of the forum, some of the hostile crowd affirmed my courage. Others left to only vandalize the church I pastored.

I learned a lot that night. I learned that life can be scary. I learned that God equips the called and gives courage to the obedient. I learned that courage isn't the absence of fear, but the recognition that something is more compelling than the source of the fear.

FEAR FACTORS

Assessing the truth of our circumstances provides the best ground for cultivating courage in our lives. Our genetics, our parents, and our past, all contribute to how we handle fear.

ASSESSING THE TRUTH OF OUR CIRCUMSTANCES PROVIDES THE BEST GROUND FOR CULTIVATING COURAGE IN OUR LIVES. OUR GENETICS, OUR PARENTS, AND OUR PAST ALL CONTRIBUTE TO HOW WE HANDLE FEAR.

God created us complex. We have bodies and souls deeply integrated into a meaningful whole person. Just as we inherit physical traits from our parents, we also inherit soulish traits from them. Our personalities, emotions, and mental faculties all have a tie to our parents.[21] We can look at our personalities and identify traits that we share with our parents. If you suffer from chronic anxiety, it is likely one of your parents suffers along with you.

Parenting styles can also contribute to how we handle scary situations. Doctors Charles Elliot and Laura Smith have identified three parenting styles that seem to contribute to anxious kids.

1. Over-protectors: These parents shield their kids from every imaginable stress or harm. If their kids stumble, they swoop them up before they even hit the ground. When their kids get upset, they fix the problem. Not surprisingly, their kids fail to find out how to tolerate fear, anxiety, or frustration.

2. Over-controllers: These parents micro-manage all their children's activities. They direct every detail from how they should play to what they should wear to how they solve arithmetic problems. They discourage independence and fertilize dependency and anxiety.

3. Inconsistent responders: The parents in this group provide their kids with erratic rules and limits. One day, they respond with understanding when their kids have trouble with their homework; the next day, they explode when their kids ask for help. These kids fail to discover the connection between their own efforts and a predictable outcome. Therefore, they

---

21. The traducianist believes that the immaterial traits of a person are passed along through parental lines. For more on this, head here:
https://www.gotquestions.org/traducianism.html.

feel that they have little control over what happens in life. It's no wonder that they feel anxious![22]

Traumatic experiences can also contribute to our fear factors. Some of my best summers were spent as a lifeguard at public beaches. I loved the water and the time outside. I watched as many people would swim without a care in the world. However, others were terrified of the water. Usually, this came from some traumatic experience in their past.

Trauma has a way of lodging in your brain like a deep splinter. It reminds you, "Hey! This hurt! Don't do that again!" Life presents many opportunities for those negative lessons. Overcoming fear and anxiety may involve a lengthy process of rewiring those places in our brain and soul that scream internally and often manifest physically through shaking, sweating, and other outward signs.

God can heal that trauma and your brain can create new pathways so that swimming (or other fear-inducing activities) can feel normal instead of fearful. We have an entire chapter for those who have trauma-based anxiety. Yet to begin the process of overcoming our fears, we must identify wrong thinking.

---

22. Charles H. Elliott and Laura L. Smith, *Overcoming Anxiety for Dummies* (Hoboken, NJ: Wiley, 2010), Kindle, 61.

IDENTIFY, VERIFY, FEATHER

Flying a twin-engine airplane has many advantages. They can fly faster and higher than most single engine airplanes. They have an extra engine if one fails (provided you haven't run out of fuel)! However, they potentially have one very fatal flaw: If one engine fails, the other produces thrust at an angle that can flip the airplane into an uncontrollable dive toward the earth.

When teaching a new student to fly a twin, we drill into their brain a procedure that we hope lives in the same place as "Mary had a little lamb." We want them to be able to recall the procedure in the scariest, most life-threatening situation they will likely ever experience.

The procedure begins with establishing positive control above a critical airspeed. Then we power up all the controls. Further, we clean up the aircraft by bringing the gear and flaps up. Next, we *identify* the bad engine. This is so critical because we don't want to shut down the *good* engine. We finish by *verifying* the bad engine and we adjust the propellor on the bad engine to produce as little drag as possible.

The Bible places a premium on good thinking. It calls us to renew our minds with new, better patterns (see Romans 12:2). It calls us to "take captive every thought to make it obedient to Christ" (2 Corinthians 10:5). God calls us to think on things that are true, noble, right, pure, lovely, and admirable (see Philippians

4:8). We are instructed to "Set your minds on things above, not on earthly things" (Colossians 3:2).

When dealing with anxiety, regardless of its source, we must identify the faulty thinking that drives the fear. Then adjust our thoughts to reflect the reality around us and let the good and true thoughts drive our lives.

As psychologists, Edmund Bourne and Lorna Garano remind us: "The truth is that it's what we say to ourselves (the self-talk of our thought life) in response to any particular situation that mainly determines our mood and feelings."[23]

9 WAYS OF WRONG, FEARFUL THINKING

1. All-or-nothing thinking. If you're not perfect or if you get anything wrong, you're a total failure.

2. Overgeneralizing. "I always do that." Or "Nothing ever works out for me."

3. Wrong focus. You pick out a single negative detail and dwell on it. You can have many great gifts, but you focus on the ones you *don't* have. I passed my last FAA check ride with flying colors, but I performed *one thing* wrong. It still bothers me, but it doesn't debilitate me. Failure isn't fatal, it's feedback.

---

23. Edmund J. Bourne and Lorna Garano, *Coping with Anxiety* (Oakland, CA: New Harbinger, 2003), 44, emphasis original. Cited in James Porter Moreland, *Finding Quiet: My Story of Overcoming Anxiety and the Practice That Brought Peace,* (Grand Rapids, MI: Zondervan, 2019), Kindle, 216.

4. Discounting the positive. If you did a good job, you tell yourself that anyone could have done it. Or the Christian response, "It's all God." Well, no, it wasn't *that good!*

5. Negative interpretations. You interpret others' actions, tone of voice, or body language in a negative way or, you assume and predict that others don't like you and that things will turn out badly. This kills relationships. If you can take a statement or action multiple ways, take it the best way.

6. Magnification or catastrophizing. You exaggerate your weaknesses or the harmful aspects of events that have happened or may happen, thus minimizing your strengths or the odds that the event will never happen and, even if it did, the results won't be that bad. "I will *die* if I speak in front of people!" You might wish you were dead, but you won't die. Most imagined catastrophes never happen.

7. Emotional reasoning. You believe that reality is the way you feel. Feelings help us understand the world, but they do not dictate reality. Dallas Willard reminds us, "Feelings have a crucial role in life, but they must not be taken as a basis for action or character change. That role falls to insight, understanding, and conviction of truth."[24]

---

24. Dallas Willard, *Renovation of the Heart: Putting on the Character of Christ,* (Colorado Springs, CO: NavPress, 2002), 138. Cited in James Porter Moreland, *Finding Quiet: My Story of Overcoming Anxiety and the Practice That Brought Peace,* (Grand Rapids, MI: Zondervan, 2019), Kindle, 216.

8. Self-labeling. "I made a mistake, so I am a loser." No, making mistakes is normal. You don't drown by falling in water, you drown by staying there.

9. Self-blame. You blame yourself for events outside your control. Some things you just cannot control. Focus on what you can change and then adjust your sails for the wind you cannot control. [25]

Do any of these faulty ways of thinking sound familiar?

These negative ways of thinking evolve into beliefs about us and the world around us. They can then become our self-talk. Our words become a rudder that steers our lives. Fear, anxiety, and worry now control our lives instead of the call and empowering of God.

Beware of extreme words, such as never, always, absolute, forever, unceasing, and constant, because they're quick and easy and they add emotional punch. But these terms have insidious downsides: They push your thinking to extremes, and your emotions join the ride. Furthermore, all-or-none words detract from coping and problem-solving.[26]

Let's look at a game plan that will place you on solid ground when fighting the fear battle.

---

25. Moreland, *Finding Quiet,* 75.
26. Elliott and Smith, *Overcoming Anxiety for Dummies,* 111.

FOUR-STEP GAME PLAN

Just like the plan for the multi-engine pilot, you must train yourself to respond to fear in healthy ways. The four-step process is: identify, verify, amplify, and solidify.

Identify the faulty belief or thought. Winning the battle includes identifying *false ideas.* The most dangerous thing in the world is a lie you believe is true. Someone defined fear as false ideas appearing real. Truth sets us free, lies keep us bound. We act on things we think are true. But if what we believe is not true, like walking on thin ice, it will have no power to sustain us in a real world. Dr. J. P. Moreland describes the process like this,

> The trick is to learn to become aware of them instead of letting them be present but under the radar and to start disempowering the message by labeling it a false brain habit triggered by a groove in your brain with no connection to reality. It is habituated distorted thinking that, through repetition of negative self-talk, has now dug a deep groove in your brain, a rut that is triggered largely through habit. It is important, then, to exert the effort to go through your day and become more aware of the presence of these messages than you have been.[27]

Ask God to help you. Psalm 139:23-24 states, "Search me, God, and know my heart; test me and know my anxious thoughts. See if there is any offensive way in me and lead me in the way

---

27. Moreland, *Finding Quiet,* 72.

everlasting." Once you *identify* the faulty way of thinking, now *verify* the truth.

VERIFY THE TRUTH

When we verify something, we establish its truth. *Verify* comes from the Latin, *verus,* meaning *true.* Instead of just telling ourselves to "stop thinking like that," we must replace the error with truth, like removing the air from a glass by filling it with water.

Each of us will trend toward certain patterns of bad thinking. Use the list to identify it and name it out loud. "No, that is catastrophizing. I am making a false prediction that (insert worst case scenario here) will happen." "No, that is a negative interpretation. Larry didn't mean to ignore me; he likely is distracted or didn't see me." "No, I am not a loser because I failed. I am a learner and will continue to learn."

Dr. Moreland, who himself struggled with debilitating anxiety frames it this way, "You say to your distorted thought, 'I know who you are. You are just a habit, a false habit that I can actually name. You are an example of emotional reasoning. You have nothing to do with reality, and I'm not going to waste my time entertaining you. I have better things to do right now. So, good-bye!'"[28]

---

28. Moreland, *Finding Quiet,* 76-77.

If we tend toward negatively interpreting the motives or words of others, doctors Bourne and Garano give this advice for verifying the truth:

> In the long run, you are probably better off making no inferences at all about people's internal thoughts. Either believe what they tell you or hold no belief at all until some conclusive evidence comes your way. Treat all your notions about people as hypotheses to be tested and checked out by asking them. Sometimes you can't check out your interpretations. For instance, you may not be ready to ask your daughter if her withdrawal from family life means she's pregnant or taking drugs. But you can allay your anxiety by generating alternative interpretations of her behavior. Perhaps she's in love. Or premenstrual. Or studying hard. Or depressed about something. By generating a string of possibilities, you may find a more neutral interpretation that is more likely to be true than your direst suspicions.[29]

AMPLIFY A NEW THOUGHT OR ACTION

Now take that truth and *amplify* it through a new focus or action. Begin to act on that truth. A young friend of mine was terribly afraid of dogs. Not because of past trauma but the thoughts of possible trauma (magnifying and emotional reasoning). When he came to my house, he had to deal with two dogs. One that didn't have the energy to bite (he was old); and

---

29. Bourne and Garano, *Coping with Anxiety,* 67.

another that would only bite if you ran (she was a special-needs border collie and would mistake you for an escaping sheep)!

As he arrived, we held the dogs back as he emotionally processed the inevitable. Little by little, each dog came to him and licked his face until the fear subsided. My friend amplified the truth that these dogs would not hurt him through a new focus away from the fear and decisive action that drowned those thoughts in a new reality.

SOLIDIFY YOUR HOPE

If you have given your life to God through Christ, you have many promises of his guidance and protection to call your own. There is no substitute for memorizing and thinking deeply upon these promises so that hope built on Christ can *solidify* in your life. Here are a few I lean on.

John 14:27: "Peace I leave with you; my peace I give you. I do not give to you as the world gives. Do not let your hearts be troubled and do not be afraid."

John 16:33: "I have told you these things, so that in me you may have peace. In this world you will have trouble. But take heart! I have overcome the world."

Philippians 4:4-7: "Rejoice in the Lord always. I will say it again: Rejoice! Let your gentleness be evident to all. The Lord is near. Do not be anxious about anything, but in every situation, by prayer and petition, with thanksgiving, present your requests to God. And the peace of God, which transcends all understanding, will guard your hearts and your minds in Christ Jesus."

Only Jesus is uniquely qualified to bring hope to a person's life. If you try to place your hope in other things, they will fall woefully short. If you place your hope in material possessions, then you will become frustrated because you will always want more than you can afford. If you *can* afford them, you will become disillusioned because the hope they promised never came.

If your hope is in yourself—then you must control everything. You will become demanding and controlling either by force or by passive-aggressive tactics. The world is too big and complex to be controlled.

If you place your hope in another person, then you will tend to be dependent upon them and your primary motivation won't be love but rather fear of loss. Actions based on unhealthy fear and co-dependency are demeaning. You were never meant to be completed or made whole by another human. Only God can do that.

For one to have hope, the provider of hope must be able to take care of the guilt and regrets of our past, make our present meaningful, and our future secure. Only Jesus can do that.

We all have regrets. Guilt and shame can debilitate the soul. However, through his grace, Jesus forgives my sin. He took my sin on the cross so I wouldn't have to carry the regret. When we sin, if we confess our sin, he is faithful to forgive us. Only Christianity offers a God that is both just and loving. He poured out his justice on Jesus so he could be free to offer us grace.

Jesus makes my present meaningful because even the mundane things in life can be lifted up to God in worship. He takes every deed done in love and makes it eternally significant. You don't have to strive for meaning, God infuses everything you do in his name with purpose. If your moments, no matter how ordinary, are connected to the eternal King of glory, you will find richness, purpose, meaning, and intimacy like you always longed for. God can take ordinary things and make something majestic out of them, because he can attach them to his eternal purposes and to the story of redemption he is unfolding throughout all generations.

Colossians 3:23-24 states: "Whatever you do, work at it with all your heart, as working for the Lord, not for human masters, since you know that you will receive an inheritance from the Lord as a reward. It is the Lord Christ you are serving."

Jesus can uniquely secure your future. He has conquered death, so death cannot rob you of anything of value. Heaven will bring a restoration of lost lives and loves all kept secure by his power and glory.

When I place my hope in that which is greater than me in every way, great enough to secure my future, great enough to love me through my imperfections, great enough to pay my infinite debt I owed to the Father, great enough to adopt me into his family and commission me to make a difference for him around the world, I can be free to love—free to love imperfect people, free to love and forgive myself, and free to love those who aren't like me—even free to love my enemies. And perfect love casts away fear (see I John 4:18).

Because Jesus loves you and is extraordinarily powerful, you can *take whatever your anxiety is trying to protect and give it to him to guard.* His grace is sufficient for you (see 2 Corinthians 12:9). If God leads you to a place of fear, know that he will give you the grace to walk through it with his peace. Without him, we should be scared! But with him, we have rest.

> Praise be to the God and Father of our Lord Jesus Christ! In his great mercy he has given us new birth into a living hope through the resurrection of Jesus Christ from the dead, and into an inheritance that can never perish, spoil or fade. This inheritance is kept in heaven for you, who through faith are shielded by God's power until the coming of the salvation that is ready to be revealed in the last time. In all this you greatly rejoice, though now for a little while you may have had to suffer grief in all kinds of trials. (I Peter 1:3-6)

Take the time to internalize the truths of this chapter and you will see your mind and heart filled with the courage and peace of God.

CHAPTER NINE

That Hurt

The process of identifying the wrong voice and amplifying the correct voice is vital to our ongoing mental health. As we renew our minds, our perspectives and attitudes become clearer and healthier. However, there may be more healing that needs to happen as you renew your mind and move on to stepping into scary spaces.

Trauma can impact our brains and souls in deep and profound ways. Abuse, abandonment, war, and even some careers can bring you into a place of injury. God designed the family to be the best place for the nurturing of children. However, when those individuals God designed to protect and provide for you become the ones who bring harm and hurt into your life, the wounds can run deep. Our fears can rise as protective mechanisms when triggered by these wounds and memories. I've asked my wife, Kim, a social worker, and certified trauma parenting specialist to write this chapter about the healing God can bring out of traumatic experiences that often trigger anxiety and fear.

Jesus has the power to reach into your heart and bring healing to the deepest parts of you. You may not forget what happened, but the pain and reactions no longer have to dominate your thoughts and feelings. Philippians 4:6-7 tells us, "Do not be anxious about anything, but in every situation, by prayer and petition, with thanksgiving, present your requests to God. And the peace of God, which transcends all understanding, will guard your hearts and minds in Christ Jesus." Jesus can guard *both* our hearts and minds.

We would be negligent in our discussion of fear if we didn't talk about real trauma and the aftermath of recovery from fear and anxiety that comes for so many people through traumatic events. According to the National Council on Behavioral Health, some 70% of adults in the United States have experienced at least one traumatic event in their life. When you work out the number, that leads to a staggering 223.4 million people![30]

Let's start with the basic understanding of trauma. Trauma occurs when a person is overwhelmed by events or circumstances and responds with intense fear, horror, and helplessness. Extreme stress overwhelms the person's capacity to cope.

There is a direct correlation between trauma and physical health conditions such as diabetes, COPD, heart disease, cancer, and high blood pressure. Trauma can come from many different places at many different developmental stages as either a child or adult. Children can suffer abuse or neglect at the hands of their

---

30. "How to Manage Trauma," *Trauma-Infographic. National Council for Behavioral Health.* Accessed June 1, 2021. www.TheNationalCouncil.org.

caregivers. Both children and adults are often victims of violence of war in countries of unrest. All too common are crimes of sexual or physical assault and so many more traumatizing events.

While generalized fear and anxiety is challenging, for many who have suffered through traumatic events, there is a very real physiological response that grips them when they seek to move past the event and move on with living. The mind may be willing, but the body can put up a resistance in the form of a fight, flight, or freeze response. Our basic biology can work against us and create barriers to freedom from fear that we need to work through.

I (Kim, Carey's wife) had the privilege of meeting a young woman and walking with her through healing after hearing her story of horrific child abuse. She was not just a survivor but someone who wanted more than anything to use her story of childhood trauma and sexual abuse to help others.

Through the years, she had gone to many different places to find healing and emotional wholeness. However, whenever she found herself stressed or frightened with certain relationships or circumstances, her brain would kick into overdrive and her dissociative self took over.

What did that look like? It often felt like you were talking to different people. One moment I would be looking into the eyes of a defeated woman, the next, she was the life of the party and could barely make eye contact because she was busy having fun or working through a million things to do.

When her stress coping skills became overwhelmed by people or life, she found herself in this crazy pattern that was not only harmful, but also dangerous because it was filled with memory blackouts and alcohol for coping. While her heart had made the decision to move forward in life, her brain and body were struggling. As someone who has worked in the field of childhood trauma and raised children with a history of complex trauma, I know that it can feel very frustrating to move forward when the past continually creeps into the present. There are a couple of critical components to remember along the way.

First, you are not broken. You are a survivor of something traumatic that happened TO you. Too often we look at survivors of trauma with the wrong lens of "what's wrong with you?" instead of "what happened to you?" The fact that you are reading this chapter is a testament to both the grace of God and your resiliency to overcome! One of the most important pieces of healing will be understanding a healthy identity in Christ. Not only has Christ redeemed your past, he made you an overcomer and a legitimate member of his family. You belong in the family and are not a problem, or a mistake. However, it's very important to understand the impact that trauma had on the lens through which you view yourself, relationships, and the world in general.

In childhood trauma, we teach foster parents that every child walks into a home with an "invisible suitcase."[31] The invisible suitcase is filled with the beliefs they have about themselves, the people who care for them, and the world in general. We equip parents with this because they must work to help upend those messages that are untrue and replace them with the messages that are true.

For example, chronic abuse and neglect from a caregiver teaches a child to believe that they are unlovable. A parent must push back when the child's words or behaviors reflect that message and replace it with a true message: "You are worthy of love." It takes a great deal of time and love to change this but it's the beauty of healing. The same is true with our thought patterns as adults.

The young woman I just mentioned consistently had difficulty believing that people would accept and love her with all the messy pieces of her life. One day while responding to her struggle and shame-filled texts, I felt the Spirit of God whisper to my heart: "Tell her she is worthy of your time and love." Through Jesus, we have been made new. His gift of love and righteousness means we don't have to carry around past labels or identities. We must learn to push back against false truths, destructive ideas, and identities that violate the truth of Scripture.

---

31. "The Invisible Suitcase: Meeting the Needs of Traumatized Children." 2016 *Trauma-Informed Parenting: Supplemental Resources.* (Adapted from Caring for Children Who Have Experienced Trauma, a Workshop for Resourcing Parents)

In the Christian world, we call it renewing our mind. This process will be SO very important in your healing from trauma.

Second, you must be patient with yourself IN the process. In the social work field, we call this self-compassion and most of us aren't usually very good at this. It's always easier for us to extend compassion to other people who are working hard and toward wholeness but become very frustrated with ourselves when our own freedom takes longer than what we anticipated.

In her book, *Self-Compassion: The Proven Power of Being Kind to Yourself,* author Kristen Neff says: "Insecurity, anxiety, and depression are incredibly common in our society, and much of this is due to self-judgment, to beating ourselves up when we feel we aren't winning in the game of life."[32] One thing that life has taught me is that God is always moving us toward wholeness and becoming the best version of ourselves. Thus, our healing is less of an arrival to an end goal and more of becoming a man or woman with deep spiritual and emotional roots and good healthy fruit that embodies a picture of maturity and wholeness.

Our scars are usually still evident and can be scraped from time to time, but it should hurt less as we allow Jesus to cleanse and cover our wounds. If we don't recognize our need for wholeness, we'll continue to bump into insecurity, anxiety, and depression our whole lives.

---

32. Kristen Neff, *Self-Compassion; The Proven Power of Being Kind to Yourself (NY: HarperCollins, 2011).*

I tell parents in trauma training that one of the best things they can do to facilitate healing in their children is to create capacity in their lives and family to attend to those wounds. Our culture doesn't give us the natural break in life, and I think that's why God has instructed us to "Be still and know that I am God" (Psalm 46:10). Our nature is to limp along in life until we are finally forced to deal with our suitcase. It will take time but healing and wholeness are the prize. If you invest in the short run, you will reap the benefits in the long run. It takes extra time and space to seek God for understanding and build supports in your life that facilitate wholeness. So where do we start?

FIND THE COURAGE TO FACE YOUR PAIN

The first critical step to healing is being willing to face the pain of your past. Most of us spend our lives trying to avoid pain, so this is naturally easier said than done. Every parent knows that our children cry and pull away when we have to clean out their wounds. Why do they do this? Because it hurts to clean it out and so they pull away from us. As people who've been through terrible things, we can convince ourselves that the dull pain of our unattended wound is easier to live with than the shorter, intensive cleaning of the Holy Spirit to our deep wounds. Unfortunately, our refusal in the short run to let healing come means consequences for the long run in the form of continued struggle, frustration, manifestation of anxiety, or other physiological symptoms that hinder your life daily. It's the classic pay-now or pay-later philosophy.

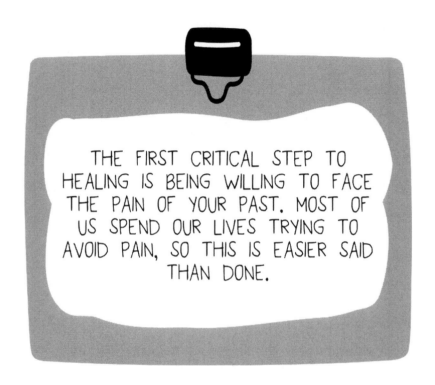

THE FIRST CRITICAL STEP TO HEALING IS BEING WILLING TO FACE THE PAIN OF YOUR PAST. MOST OF US SPEND OUR LIVES TRYING TO AVOID PAIN, SO THIS IS EASIER SAID THAN DONE.

The enemy of our soul is allowed to continue to afflict what Christ has given us freedom from. When you consider the opportunities for joy and relationship that are wide open for us, I hope you'll see that the trade-off is worth it. I am, however, not suggesting you do this alone. Equally important to pursuing healing and wholeness is to create a support system to help you do this. You will need a team of people who will help you when the pain feels too much to bear.

Every one of us has different needs but I think it's important to have the following in common: a trustworthy and godly counselor who can help you implement healing tools when the battle of the past is raging; spiritual mentors who understand trauma and patience to walk through your healing, continually reminding you of truth; friends who have walked similar roads and can remind you that the end is worth pulling back the wounds so healing can be complete; and a local church community that can give you a safe place to belong and challenge you to grow into the son or daughter Jesus intended you to be from the very beginning.

The role of your counselor will be critical, so I encourage people to take time to choose wisely someone who foundationally believes that Jesus heals and sets us free. There are many tools, but it is most important to focus on the One who brings the healing. Jesus gives us wisdom to develop helpful techniques, but there is no process that completes our healing or replaces the Person of Jesus. He is the only one who can ground our identity, set our value, and guard our security.

Dr. Bruce Perry, childhood trauma expert, alludes to the importance of relationships in the healing process from trauma: "Relationships matter: the currency for systemic change was trust, and trust comes through forming healthy working relationships. People, not programs, change people."[33]

Even secular science knows that healing requires relationships, and there is no greater relationship than the one you have with Jesus. During this time, you will discover a wonderful and faithful Father who is passionate about your healing and committed to your wholeness. His heart is something you can trust and hold tightly to when fear creeps in and tries to sabotage your recovery. This will be your anchor throughout the process. Your counselor should encourage this as the central goal of your healing and hopefully, walk in step with the Spirit of God as you discover painful parts of the past that may be controlling you.

Counselors have many tools they bring to the table. It would be impossible to create an exhaustive list of resources here; nor do I perfectly know which tools you need. However, let me mention a few tools that have become commonplace in the world of trauma-informed care.

The Church has often been resistant to talk about mental health struggles and even more resistant to acknowledge that people sometimes need more than a quick prayer and parting Scripture to be better. I think we can retraumatize people when we do this. We reinforce the deception that THEY are broken

---

33. B. D. Perry and M. Szalavitz, *The Boy Who Was Raised as a Dog: And Other Stories from A Child Psychiatrist's Notebook*. (NY: Basic Books, 2007).

when they are unable to "pick themselves up by their bootstraps"—and this should change.

Many trauma-survivors weren't fortunate to have the developmental bootstraps that the rest of us had and their life experiences forced them to compensate to survive. When the mind, for example, is caught up in the darkness of depression, it can be too hard to fight off the interference of despair. When the interference of past trauma is hounding people day after day, there is a time to gather tools to empower them to begin the process of freedom. If we demonize tools (medication, counseling, grounding exercises, etc.) we often leave them tormented by the trauma of their past.

God has given us godly people who've spent years researching different forms of healing to help set people up for success. Many of the tools are actually God-ideas! Mindfulness is simply a form of meditation that God himself called his people to practice so they never forget his promises. Read Psalm 1 for example.

Grounding exercises (that help us focus on the here and now) are anchors of truth to keep us focused in the present so we aren't tied to the trauma of our past or carried away with anxiety for all that the future brings (Matthew 6:34). Grounding is a God-idea that helps us stay rooted in the present where Christ has called us to live. Different forms of psychotherapy, like EMDR (Eye Movement Desensitization and Reprocessing) or TF-CBT (Trauma-Focused Cognitive Behavioral Therapy are just a few tools that help people, in a safe environment, reorganize and make sense of the past, and enable them to calm the amygdala (the trauma center of the brain).

EMDR is a structured therapy that encourages the patient to briefly focus on the trauma memory while simultaneously experiencing bilateral stimulation (typically eye movements), which is associated with a reduction in the vividness and emotion associated with the trauma memories.[34]

In his book, *Finding Quiet*, J.P. Moreland shares about the power of EMDR therapy (under the careful eye of his Christian counselor) to help him deal with the debilitating memories of his past that kept anxiety a reality in his life. He says this:

> EMDR involves a technique discovered almost by chance in 1987 that helps get to isolated, painful memories whose brain grooves are so deep and isolated that ordinary talk therapy may not reach them. In fact, during my EMDR therapy, I experienced memories I hadn't recalled in more than sixty years, and when I did, I was able to connect them with other memories, feel and acknowledge the events recalled, release them, and integrate the memories with the rest of my life.[35]

We must, as the Church, begin to safely allow people the space to bring their pain into the light and talk about hard things so Jesus can help them put the pieces of their soul back together. He doesn't erase our memories, but he does allow us to put them

---

34. L. Maxfield and R. M. Solomon, "Eye Movement Desensitization and Reprocessing (EMDR) Therapy." *American Psychological Association,* May 2017, Accessed December 2021. https://www.apa.org/ptsd-guideline/treatments/eye-movement-reprocessing.

35. Moreland, *Finding Quiet,* 130-131.

to rest in our minds AND body. This is powerfully consistent with the teaching of James Chapter 5:16, that confession, along with the prayers of God's people, powerfully facilitates our healing. Whatever it takes, find the courage to bring the pain of your past into the light so that you can move forward.

BREAK THE SILENCE

For victims of trauma, the greatest violation is often that of losing their voice. Their voice gives them the power to say "NO." Their voice gives them the ability to ask for help. Voice is a God-given design that gives us power to protect us. Voice also gives validity to your loss. I don't think it's ironic that a voice and language is one of the distinguishing marks as image-bearers and when we lose that power, it can leave us feeling diminished. There is great power to free us from fear and the past when we open our mouths with words to express our pain.

Unfortunately, the world is filled with people who never listen. While this is tragic, it's also an opportunity for the church to create space for people to rediscover their voice. In fact, Proverbs 31:8-9 talks about the power of God's people to stand in the gap on behalf of those who can't seem to find their own voice.

Proverbs 31:8-9 states: "Speak up for those who cannot speak for themselves, for the rights of all who are destitute. Speak up and judge fairly; defend the rights of the poor and needy."

We, as the church, should be willing to speak up until others are able. There have been times in our ministry when we've had to make hard phone calls or intercede when someone is being victimized. Love sometimes requires this.

The Church should also be a haven of safe listening. During a recent course on trauma-informed aftercare, I ran across something called "The Safe Listener's Promise" and it has impacted me greatly. By nature, I am a fixer. If something or someone is broken, my first reaction is to talk and my second, is to fix. But after reading this and learning more about helping others heal from trauma, I realized that it's easy to get in the way of healing when I do that. Here are the goals:

I will listen to understand.

I will keep what you share private.

I will not minimize your pain.

I will not compare your pain with my own.

I will not give quick solutions.

I will listen again when you want to share more.

While people need our support, love, and care, we want to create space for Jesus to do the proper and permanent healing that is necessary.

LAMENT OUR LOSS

Just like listening, another helpful tool that is critical to the healing and freedom from trauma-related fear is the lament. Hurt comes into our lives because we had expectations that were left unmet or worse, betrayed. Many of those expectations were based on our God-given needs. To lament is to wail, moan, cry, or sob; to offer a complaint. When our hearts are hurt or broken over these unmet expectations, it's an important part of our healing process to vocalize our loss and lift our complaint heavenward. The Scriptures are filled with laments, including the Psalms and an entire book of Lamentations. The shortest verse of the Bible is a lament: "Jesus wept." What does God feel about your hurt, your loss, your abuse? He weeps.

The world is broken presently because of sin, and sin breaks people. God promises that it won't always be this way but until the culmination of God's final redemptive act, we live in the tension of a broken place. Created in his image, he feels our pain deeply and invites us to take the hurt, pain, and loss from the inside and lift the weight of that burden up to God outside so we can stand up unburdened and unhindered from the pain and fear of this past. The Trauma Healing Institute (THI) offers a wonderful road map for learning the practice of lamenting based on Psalm 13:

How long, Lord? Will you forget me forever?
How long will you hide your face from me?
How long must I wrestle with my thoughts

and day after day have sorrow in my heart?
How long will my enemy triumph over me?

Look on me and answer, Lord my God.
    Give light to my eyes, or I will sleep in death, and my enemy
will say, "I have overcome him,"
    and my foes will rejoice when I fall.

But I trust in your unfailing love;
    my heart rejoices in your salvation.
I will sing the Lord's praise,
    for he has been good to me.

Step 1: Call out to God.
Step 2: Tell God about your pain.
Step 3: Ask God for help.
Step 4: Affirm your trust in God.

I encourage you to integrate this process into your healing journey. There is something that happens to us when we stop trying to ignore our pain and really take the time to complete this process of lamenting our pain. I think it has a lot to do with this process of moving in close to God to tell him what's hurting your heart. When you move in close to God, he touches you, and you're never the same.

EMBRACE THE POWER OF FORGIVENESS

C.S. Lewis writes, "Everyone says forgiveness is a lovely idea until they have something to forgive." Most of us can connect with this struggle. Most of the time we are good, and we have no problem letting go and forgiving. But then there are the other times, the 5% of the time, where it's just plain hard! I've discovered in my own life that there is often a correlation between the closeness and expectations I had in the relationship and my difficulty forgiving the person. This can help us understand how it's even harder when it comes to traumatic events that have happened!

Unforgiveness can be a real barrier for all of us. One of the most important things to remember is that unforgiveness will change us if we continue to hold on to it. When we carry unforgiveness and the corresponding toxic emotions like anger, resentment, and bitterness, it poisons us, and we lose sight of reality. It also becomes a prison for us. The irony of unforgiveness is that in refusing to let it go, we allow it to torture us and the people around us that we love, instead of the one who hurt us.

Jesus taught frequently about this principle of walking in forgiveness and how it was essential to our spiritual well-being. He knew the power of unforgiveness (just like other sins) to deceive, mock, and exploit us. He knew it would be used to keep us bound to the past and to those people who hurt us. So, he made sure he was clear on the importance of forgiving.

While it might be hard, here are a few things we must remember: Forgiveness is not saying that the injustice was okay. You are choosing to let them off your hook, but they are never off God's hook unless they have an encounter with Christ and allow him to free them from their own guilt.

Forgiveness does not mean that what happened did not hurt. But instead, it recognizes that to continue to hold on to this allows them to continue hurting you. Revisiting the hurt and internally building your case against the person over and over doesn't heal you but it holds you.

Forgiveness is not continuing in an abusive relationship. In fact, love does not tolerate abuse or ill-treatment; rather love acts for the good of others.

Forgiveness does not require that the offender apologize or even change their behavior. Regardless of whether there is repentance on the part of the other person, you can still be free. Embracing forgiveness unshackles us from the power and prison of our past and transfers responsibility for justice to the place it belongs—in God's capable hands.

REPLACE THE LIES

Up until now, all these steps to freedom from fear dealt with the past. Now comes the hard work of the present! Much of the work and freedom that we need will be in reframing our thoughts, beliefs, and then ultimately, our actions. Remember that invisible suitcase? We must stop coming into agreement with the lies of our past hurts and wounds. Counseling will help us discuss the pain of our past, but it's the Word of God that helps us recognize those deceptive messages.

There is a story in John 5:2-8 about a man who had been an invalid for 38 years. In this story, Jesus finds the man lying next to the pool of Bethesda desperately wanting to get well but failing. Jesus asked the man this question: "Do you want to get well?" What kind of question is that to ask a man lying next to a healing pool trying to get in day after day? One thing the Scriptures have taught me is that when Jesus asks a question, it's not because he needs information, but because we need information! There was a helplessness portrayed in this story that I think Jesus was trying to help the man (and us) see so we could understand the power of ownership we must take in our own healing.

Prior to Christ, we create a lens and narrative that is based not on the truth, but on lies from our past experiences. This often gets us in trouble or creates habits that are destructive to us. If you continue to read the story of this man in John chapter five, you discover that Jesus found him later, after his healing and celebration, and said "Stop sinning or something worse may happen to you."

You see, to find freedom from pain and our deep fears, there must be a decision to recalibrate our thoughts to come into agreement with truth. If we try to seek wholeness apart from the truth, we continue to be susceptible to the enemy's bondage. How has your trauma impacted you or altered the lens through which you view life? Determine to allow the Holy Spirit the freedom to begin to transform those destructive lies about you with the truth of your place in God's family, the kind of Father God is, and more.

As we replace those negative thoughts with the truth of God's Word, taking hold of those lies that are destructive, we are giving Jesus permission and authority to repack our suitcase and transform our thoughts, beliefs, and actions—which in turn transforms our minds, body, and soul—bringing us into a place of integrated wholeness. There is no shortcut to this process, and it will take the help of your support team to help you. The good news is that while there isn't a shortcut, there IS grace as you relearn and repack your heart and mind with the truth.

SHARE YOUR STORY

The last step in wholeness is being willing to share your story. When God redeems your story, repacks your heart and mind, and restores your voice, you have an opportunity to help others in their journey to find healing from trauma. As I indicated earlier in this chapter, sin breaks people and consequently, the world is filled with hurting and comfortless people. Our lives become a testimony of what God can do. We often discover that the same comfort that God gave to us, he'll use through us to heal others.

OUR LIVES BECOME A TESTIMONY OF WHAT GOD CAN DO. WE OFTEN DISCOVER THAT THE SAME COMFORT THAT GOD GAVE TO US, HE'LL USE THROUGH US TO HEAL OTHERS.

Revelation 12:11 says: "They triumphed over him by the blood of the Lamb and by the word of their testimony; they did not love their lives so much as to shrink from death."

This Scripture depicts a spiritual battle *of all battles* and a declaration of war by the enemy of our soul on the Bride of Christ. We see two things that are critical to overcoming. First, the power of the blood of Jesus Christ. When Jesus went to the cross, He made the way for you and me to move from a position of slave to sin like an outcast or orphan to a permanent place in the family. This transition from powerless to position is made possible because of the blood of Jesus. But something else happens when we, with our own mouth, declare the transforming power of Christ to heal in our lives. It is powerful because it invites others to consider the possibility that God can change their life, too! When your story is told, you can plant seeds of hope in so many other people and it encourages you all over again. Only Jesus can make that happen! It's the power of redemption!

One last thing to remember. Even though I've given you these "points" in a particular order, please know that these are fluid, and you may have to move back and forth between them multiple times or revisit certain areas again during certain seasons or situations that are particularly triggering. Don't let that discourage you! I have found that human beings tend to make idols out of the process. But God operates differently. He says: "I need you to learn to trust in me and not in a process." Every healing Jesus did was unique, but the common thread was Jesus. The person of Jesus and your relationship with him is more critical to your freedom and wholeness than the process Jesus uses. So, build your team, set your face forward, and when things get rough, decide to trust Him!

CHAPTER TEN

Pick Up the Snake; Do It Scared

God heard the cry of an enslaved people and looked for a leader that could bring pressure to the dominant world power in Egypt. He found a man looking after sheep in the wilderness. Moses was raised deep in the heart of the Egyptian power structure, but he had to flee because he murdered a man. He later settled down as a shepherd. That's where a fiery bush caught his attention. God spoke to him and asked him to do one of the scariest things he could—march into the throat of Egypt and demand to let God's people go.

Moses didn't respond as a fearless man of courage. He tried to negotiate out of the task. We see Moses highlight several scary things and God answered them one-by-one. Exodus 4:1-17 gives us the account.

First, Moses pointed out his fear of not being heard, valued, and believed. "Moses answered, "What if they do not believe me or listen to me and say, 'The Lord did not appear to you'?"

Then he pointed out his fear of public speaking in verse 10: "Pardon your servant, Lord. I have never been eloquent, neither in the past nor since you have spoken to your servant. I am slow of speech and tongue."

125

During this conversation God asked Moses to perform a few tasks. One was to place his hand inside his cloak. When he removed it, his hand was white with leprosy, a deadly skin disease. He cycled it through the cloak again and it came out clear as a child's cheek. God showed his power over life and death. When you settle the death question, no other fears need to control us.

REMEMBER, COURAGE IS NOT THE ABSENCE OF FEAR, BUT THE REALIZATION THAT SOMETHING IS MORE IMPORTANT THAN FEAR.

Just before this incident God asked him to throw down his staff. As he did, it turned into a snake. (God seems to cover all the big fears in this one session, death, snakes, public speaking, being mocked, and embarrassed.) Moses did what came naturally. He ran! Then God asked him to do something crazy. To pick up the snake! God asked him to face his fears, trust his God, and *do it scared.* Remember, courage is not the absence of fear, but the realization that something is more important than fear.

Moses, catastrophized in his thinking, came up with one excuse after another as to why he couldn't fulfill his calling. But sometimes you just have to pick up the snake. Sometimes you must do it scared knowing that God has called you and he will give you the grace to handle it.

Most people are hindered from becoming champions by three imposters: fear, ignorance, and sweat—fear being chief among them. It can keep us from engaging the other two. It keeps us from learning and from trying. Fear keeps us from learning and trying new things.

Fear is a bully; it intimidates us and if we learn how to stare it down, we can pull back the curtain to see that maybe the wizard isn't so intimidating after all, especially considering what God has done in our lives.

FEAR TRAINING

Our brains consist of billions of neurons. These neurons create a dynamic circuitry that integrates deeply with our immaterial soul to help produce our personality. God designed some parts of our brain to produce feelings of stress and fear. Some fear is healthy. It preserves our lives and health. I don't wear a seatbelt because they look good or feel comfortable. I do it so my head doesn't go places it wasn't designed to go in the event of an accident.

These circuits talk to each other through electro-chemical signals. The limbic system and the frontal lobes dance together to help us navigate life with healthy boundaries around scary things. The limbic system—including the amygdala—helps us sense danger and cues our fear responses like fight or flight. The frontal lobe processes information and provides a governor of sorts so we don't make poor choices or live in a constant state of hyper-vigilant stress. It provides us with reasoning ability. Doctors Elliot and Smith explain it this way,

> The limbic system could set off alarms reflexively upon seeing a snake. However, the frontal lobes may signal the system to calm down as it processes the fact that the snake is in a glass cage. In anxiety disorders, either the limbic system or the frontal lobes (or both) may fail to function properly. . . . Thus, the limbic system may trigger fear responses too easily and too often, or the frontal lobes may fail to use logic to quell the fears set off by the limbic system.[36]

It's as if you have a two-pilot cockpit. One pilot is hyper-vigilant and is ready to enact the emergency procedures at a moment's notice. This is your sympathetic nervous system. It triggers your fear response. You also have another pilot; he is designed to fly the plane under normal circumstances. This is

---

36. Elliott and Smith, *Overcoming Anxiety for Dummies*, Kindle, 48-49.

your para-sympathetic nervous system. It also promotes the resting, calming response after the danger has passed. In two-pilot operations it is crucial to identify the PF (pilot flying) and the PM (pilot monitoring).

In balanced living, the Pilot Flying should be your para-sympathetic system. It navigates normal life and should be in control most of the time with the sympathetic nervous system serving as the Pilot Monitoring looking for any truly dangerous situation. In unbalanced living, the two pilots have switched roles. The sympathetic nervous system has taken over the PF duties. It is in constant fight or flight mode. This kind of stress can lead to long-term health consequences. To achieve a balanced, healthy life, we must make the pilots switch seats.

Part of overcoming debilitating anxiety and fear is retraining our brain to correctly assess danger and normal risk. One cannot live life without risk. We must learn to manage our stresses so we can fulfill the call of God on our lives. Most things of note are accomplished by scared, tired people. If you follow God, he will lead you into scary situations. God is not boring. He overflows with intimacy and adventure. As author C. S. Lewis put it, he is not a tame lion, but a good one.

One of the primary goals of childhood is to figure out how to handle the scary things in life—bogeymen, thunderstorms, algebra. If a child is kept from reasonable risk by figuratively wrapping them in bubble wrap, it will prevent them from developing resilience.

In the book, *The Coddling of the American Mind*, Greg Lukianoff and Jonathan Haidt describe how parents' attempts to promote their kids' emotional well-being often instead makes them more emotionally fragile. They found that the more kids are sheltered, the more likely they will struggle with anxiety. And the less exposure they get to ideas and experiences they do not like, the more "triggered" they get by the time they arrive at college.

In fact, based on Greg's personal and professional experience as a therapist, his theory was this: Students were beginning to demand protection from speech they deemed harmful or violent because they had unwittingly learned to employ the very cognitive distortions that Cognitive Behavioral Therapy tries to correct. Stated simply: Many university students are learning to think in distorted ways, and this increases their likelihood of becoming fragile, anxious, and easily hurt.[37]

Doctors Elliot and Smith recommend exposing your kids to common phobia-inducing situations:

> If you want to prevent your children from acquiring one of these common phobias, you can inoculate them. You do that by providing safe interactions with the potentially feared event or object—prior to any fear developing. Try the following activities: Take your kids to a museum or zoo that offers hands-on experiences with snakes and insects. Climb a mountain together. Watch a storm from the safety of your living room couch. Discuss how

37. Greg Lukianoff and Jonathan Haidt, *The Coddling of the American Mind* (New York: Penguin Publishing Group, 2018), Kindle, 9.

lightning and thunder work. If you don't have a dog or cat of your own, go to the pound and visit puppies and kittens. Research has proven that this method works. For example, studies have shown that children bitten by dogs don't develop a phobia as readily if they have had past, positive experiences with dogs. Children who fly at an early age rarely develop a phobia to flying. The more experiences you provide your children with, the better their chances are of growing up without phobias. [38]

It is better to build kids for the roads than the roads for the kids. We must experience risk early in life or we can never distinguish between truly dangerous and mildly risky. One will never reach their potential if they never leave a safe space or can't deal with people and ideas that trigger them.

PICKING UP SNAKES

Therapists have found that we can create new pathways in our brain and unlearn the conditioned fear responses through a stepwise journey into scary situations. We can learn to switch the pilot seats. Cognitive behavioral therapy or exposure therapy allows you to reassociate these situations with a more calm and peaceful response. You may still experience nervousness, but

38. Elliott and Smith, *Overcoming Anxiety for Dummies*, Kindle, 305.

over time, you gain confidence and trust that these situations are not the catastrophe you imagined.

The problem with this kind of adventure is that it's uncomfortable. But you are the hero in this story! Every hero has a challenge, and this quest is yours. God told Moses over and over he could do it because God was with him. The same God is with you! Picking up snakes requires commitment to facing Pharaohs and giants—and moving with consistent courage into situations you may have avoided for years. It will involve repeated trips into Pharaoh's court until you have achieved a breakthrough of peace and freedom. This can take weeks or months. You cannot retrain years of fear in a few weeks.

THE FLIGHT LESSON

Most people when they begin flying share both excitement and trepidation. I can anticipate those who will freeze from task saturation where their brain just cannot process all that is happening. I have experienced those who have just let go of the airplane in hopes I could save us. Many times, I've had to take the controls to keep us from becoming a bad physics experiment. Incremental steps is the key to it all. We slowly push boundaries of competence until the student has the skill and judgment to fly by themselves.

Picking up snakes or exposure therapy happens in small, persistent, incremental (some would say "baby") steps. Flight training psychologists have found that pilots can develop strategies to enable high functioning during terrifying experiences. They group them into two categories, "skill-building" and "self-calming" strategies. Skill-building involves increasing exposure to challenges until one can handle the tasks under pressure. Self-calming strategies involve two critical components: physical mechanisms that trigger a relaxation response and self-talk that quickly dispels negative and faulty thinking.

SKILL-BUILDING

Skill-building begins with the end goal in mind and develops incremental steps to gradually train yourself to master your formerly phobic situations. For instance, to conquer your fear of swimming you would create a stepwise program that would build both *competence* and *confidence* as they both feed off each other.

My wife and I took scuba lessons together and it tested the fiber of our marriage. I take to the water like a fish, but she doesn't enjoy swimming and struggled with claustrophobia. The combination of the dark, weedy water mixed with a mask and regulator was not her idea of fun.

Our instructor placed my wife on a plan that would enable her to engage each step until she felt only mild to moderate anxiety. First, we swam on the surface of the water with a mask and snorkel. Then we submerged ourselves in shallow water so at any time we could stand up. Next, he held her hand in slightly deeper water, never leaving her side. With time and persistence, she eventually dove into the open ocean. (She still refuses to dive in the ocean at night, however.)

Early in your steps, you may want a support partner. I was my wife's dive partner when she finally let go of the instructor's hand. Practice each step until your anxiety level becomes manageable, then move to the next step. Understand that this is positive stress. Without stress brought about by prudent risk and adventure, we become bored, depressed, and atrophied. Like astronauts in a weightless environment, their muscles atrophy and they cannot handle the gravity of earth. They use elastic bands to stress their muscles to keep them healthy. Good stress is momentary and passing—even thrilling (think roller coasters). Bad stress is continual, unrelenting, and chronic.

In their book, *Coping with Anxiety,* doctors Bourne and Garano give a good example of a stepwise plan for conquering the fear of elevators:

1. Look at elevators, watching them come and go.
2. Stand in a stationary elevator with your support person.
3. Travel up and down one and then two floors with your support person.

4. Stand in a stationary elevator alone.

5. Travel up or down one floor alone, with your support person waiting outside the elevator on the floor where you will arrive.

6. Travel two to three floors with your support person.

7. Travel two to three floors alone, with your support person waiting outside the elevator on the floor where you will arrive.

8. Moving toward mastery, travel up or down one floor alone, with your support person waiting in a car outside the building.

9. Travel up and down one floor alone without your support person at all (that is, you've visited the building on your own).

10. Travel up and down two or three floors alone without your support person.

11. Continue to incrementally increase the number of floors you ascend on the elevator without the presence of your support person, until you can reach the top of a five- to ten-story building.

12. Continue to incrementally increase the number of floors you ascend without your support person until you can reach the top of a twenty- to thirty-story building, or the tallest building in your city with an elevator.

13. Practicing every day will increase the rate of your progress. Travel on two different elevators in two different buildings of varying heights on your own.

14. Travel on a variety of different elevators in a variety of different buildings in your city (or nearest city) on your own.[39]

SELF-CALMING STATEMENTS AND PHYSICAL STRATEGIES

Fear is both in the mind and in the body. We have autonomic responses to fear that can help us cope well with real danger or move us into a debilitated state even with a false perception of danger. We want to develop skills that can bring calm and peace to our minds and bodies during these triggered times. These come in the forms of self-talk that proclaims truth to our minds and physical actions that reform our bodies' response to our phobia.

Before I talk to myself about my situation, I talk to God about myself. I ask God to show me what my fear is trying to protect. Then I give it to God to guard. I give him my identity, my value, my fear of failure and embarrassment, my fear of pain, loss, or

---

39. Bourne and Garano, Coping with Anxiety, Kindle, 77-78.

anything else that comes to mind. I know he will guard those things forever. I pray myself in love with the people that I will potentially serve because I am free of this fear. I affirm his love and care for me by proclaiming some of my favorite verses. "Lord, I cast this fear of _____ upon you because you care for me. I am free to enjoy my life because you have set me free. And I love those you have called me to serve and perfect love casts out fear."

Then I identify any negative self-talk (see Chapter 8 for a refresher) and replace it with an affirmative statement. Make sure you create statements that feel reasonable and not completely outlandish. Some of my favorites include: "I'm here to do my best and let God do the rest." "I can do this." "God is with me." "Failure isn't fatal, it's feedback." "This cannot touch my value." "Help me to serve well." "I'm excited to do this." Allow God and your support team to help you craft your self-talk statements. Remember the tongue is a rudder, so what you say (especially to yourself) will help guide your life.

To address the physical factors of anxiety and worry, experts have found that certain techniques can calm nerves and lower heart rates. These take practice and persistence. You are retraining your body to respond in a healthy manner.

The most popular and effective techniques involve breathing and muscle relaxation. A deep breath or a series of deep breaths while focusing on something peaceful has great power to reduce anxiety. Take a deep breath in through your nose. Hold it for a few seconds, then slowly let it out through your mouth. Repeat this several times.

I use this when flying a series of takeoffs and landings called *touch and goes*. After the landing, during the rollout, I take a breath to calm myself and assess the situation before I apply power for the next takeoff. This helps reduce the anxious state I just experienced during the previous landing.

Muscle relaxation techniques involve a series of tensing and relaxing various parts of the body. Doctors Elliot and Smith outline a progression in their book on overcoming anxiety:

> Sit down in this chair, close your eyes, and relax. Pretend the floor is trying to rise up and that you have to push it back down with your legs and feet. Push, push, push. Okay, now relax your legs and feet. Notice how nice they feel. Oh, oh. The floor is starting to rise again. Push it back down. Good job, now relax. Now tighten your stomach muscles. Make your stomach into a shield of armor, strong like Superman. Hold the muscles in.
> Good, now relax. One more time; tighten those stomach muscles into steel. Hold it. Great, now relax. See how nice, warm, and relaxed your stomach feels. Now, spread your fingers and put your hands together in front of your chest. Squeeze your hands together. Push hard and use your arm muscles, too. Pretend you're squeezing Play-Doh between your hands and make it as squished as you can. Okay, now relax. Take a deep breath. Hold it. Now let the air out slowly. Again, spread your fingers wide, and squish Play-Doh between your hands. Hold it. Great. Now relax. Pretend you're a turtle. You want to go into your shell. To do that, bring your shoulders way up high and try to touch your ears with your shoulders. Feel your head go down into your shell. Hold it. Okay, now relax.

See how nice, warm, and relaxed your shoulders and neck feel. One more time now. Be a turtle and go into your shell. Hold it. Good. Now relax. Finally, squish your face up like it does when you eat something that tastes really, really bad. Squish it up tight. Hold it. Okay, now relax. Take a deep breath. Hold it. Now let the air out slowly. One more time. Squish your face up real tight. Hold it. Relax. Good job! See how limp and relaxed your body feels.

When you feel upset or worried, you can do this all by yourself to feel better. You don't have to do all the muscles like we did. You can just do what you want to.[40]

I typically don't go through all the muscle groups today. I have before and now I can just pick one or two combined with some stretches to help train my body to deal with stressful situations. In the airplane, I compress these techniques, so they don't take much time at all. A deep breath and shaking out my hands do the trick.

FLIGHT SIMULATOR

Flight simulators allow pilots to fly under stressful situations without the fear of *actually* crashing. Good simulators help build your skills and stress responses to train pilots to deal with emergencies with calmness and competence. Using your

---

40. Elliott and Smith, *Overcoming Anxiety for Dummies*, Kindle, 313-314.

imagination to visualize an upcoming situation will help you navigate it in real life.

Imagining allows us to mentally rehearse our scenario and how we should respond. This helps our brain rewire and our bodies remember. In fact, visualizing movement changes how our brain networks are organized, creating more connections among different regions. Our brains have nearly the same activity when we visualize as when we actually perform the action. Athletes and other high-performing individuals harness the power of visualization to help them perform under pressure.

One of my school sessions took me to Southern California. I had the bright idea that I would attempt to earn my Gracie Jiu Jitsu blue belt while I was out there since the academy was located nearby. I studied for a year via video, but I wanted to test with a real black belt. I arrived a day early to take a pre-test. After the pre-test, the instructor said it was likely I wouldn't pass the test the next day. I was stunned. I thought I would cancel the test and forget about it.

My kids and my wife wouldn't let me off the hook. I was afraid of embarrassing myself and wasting any more money as the test cost hundreds of dollars. The next day I went through every move I could by myself. I had no partner, so I visualized and performed each detail on the floor of my apartment. That made all the difference. I passed that evening.

Harness the power of visualization to retrain your mind and body to handle stress in a healthy way. Much of life is repetitive and you know what brings about anxiety for you. Imagine yourself in stressful situations and visualize yourself handling them with grace and peace. Do this repeatedly to help train your body and mind to handle fearful situations. God has given us the power of a sanctified imagination—use it for his glory!

Beyond traditional meditation and deep breathing, there is another tool that I (Kim) personally found very helpful in allowing me to regulate stress and anxiety during especially trying seasons of life and ministry: HeartMath.

The HeartMath Institute was founded by Doc Childre in 1991 as a research and education organization to help people balance their physical, mental, and emotional systems into balanced alignment with their heart.

Often, I would hear people in the church tell me to just "take your thoughts captive" but when anxiety threatened to overwhelm me, no matter how hard I tried to concentrate and extinguish my racing thoughts, I struggled in this area. So rather than start with the racing mind, HeartMath teaches to focus first on the heart and its rhythms. J. P. Moreland does a tremendous job outlining the theology of the heart, the overall concepts which make up a person's mind, will, emotions, and spirit, in his book, *Finding Quiet.* He lays out a quick and easy plan of integrating HeartMath into your anxiety-reducing routine to help especially with obsessive thoughts.

HeartMath is most effective when realized as one tool of a bigger toolbox to transform the heart and mind and free it from

141

the shackles of anxiety. To summarize the practical piece, it starts first with focusing your attention on the heart muscle itself—eyes closed, hand on your chest, and breathing until you feel your heart beating. This can take a while if you have significant anxiety. Be patient and wait until you feel that you are focused on that heart muscle. Then begin the process of envisioning your breathing through that heart area slowly and gently until they are in sync.

Again, this may take time as you consciously must wait until your body is in the present and aligned with your breathing. Finally, refocus by recalling a positive and God-honoring memory that came with a positive feeling such as joy, love, safety, or peace. Once you visit that memory, move to the feeling(s) associated with it.

For example, my memory takes me back to my horse ride across the state of Michigan on a particularly sunny and warm day during a ten-day trip. While most days were physically exhausting and emotionally grueling, I remember vividly this day when we left the trail for a bit to travel down a paved country road. Being in the lead, I remember my horse gaiting beautifully while I listened to the clip-clop of his hooves on the pavement. We were having a great time laughing as a group of horse girls living the dream as we gaited down that road.

This memory brings with it a feeling of fun, joy, and well-being that still makes me smile. Once I recall that memory, I move to the feelings I have and allow those feelings to flood my heart and allow it to become the focus rather than my overthinking brain or racing anxiety. Essentially, HeartMath is a type of grounding exercise among many. As you are first learning grounding techniques, you'll find it beneficial to do them more often. I found that doing this in the evenings before bed allowed me to sleep better and let go of the stress from the day. Additionally, I also added a quiet meditation on the Lord's Prayer or Psalm 23 to enhance that feeling of well-being and safety after the exercise to further reduce anxiety.

While I use this HeartMath practice as a tool, I'm not a student of the HeartMath Institute or an expert in its theories or research. I know that like meditation or other grounding exercises, the secular world can misuse or take tools to an extreme. However, when integrated in a God-honoring way, I've personally benefited from this exercise.

LET MY PEOPLE GO

Jody went to school to become a structural engineer. After graduation, he went to work in a steel company's engineering department. God began drawing him to work with youth at his church, but he had a big problem. He hated, hated, hated, to speak in public. It petrified him. He failed public speaking twice in college. His teacher, seeing little hope for Jody as a speaker told him to drop the course. But God wouldn't relent. He kept drawing him to work with teenagers.

Finally, his love and passion overcame his fear. Jody began taking steps to pick up snakes so he could help a generation live in the freedom that only Jesus can bring. God took someone who flunked public speaking twice, and now travels the country speaking at school assemblies looking to help students overcome their fears.

On one occasion, he was at a school in the south on a sweltering, early summer day and a girl sat in the bleachers dressed like it was winter. She looked out of place and distant. After the assembly, Jody and his wife Wendy went to speak with her. The girl wanted to talk but also was somewhat elusive. Finally, Wendy asked her, "Tell me about the best day in your life." The girl said it was yesterday. "Yesterday! Wow, what happened yesterday to make it the best day of your life?" "My mom got sent to prison," she answered. "Wow, what?" "Mom got sent to prison and that was the best day?" Wendy responded.

The girl began to unfold a story of a mother who was drawn into drugs and began to prostitute herself to accommodate her habit. Over time, when the drugs and lifestyle took a toll on the mother, and the men no longer wanted her, she loaded up her 10-year-old daughter and began to pimp her out. This girl was sold for drugs from age 10 to 14. Not in India, not in Bangladesh, in America.

Now Jody and Wendy help lead Freedom International with two 48-foot trailers that he designed using his engineering background, bought by money given by teenagers. With these rigs they can pull into underserved communities and partner with state and local law enforcement and the FBI, to rescue kids out of slavery. When a child is rescued, they have bunk beds to stay in temporarily. Then they fly them to a location for placement out of the region.

Because Jody picked up some snakes and faced his debilitating fear, he and his wife now make the world a less scary place for kids all around the country.

We need more heroes. The world doesn't have to be this scary. We have a God who has overcome the world, and we have a church called to rescue it. May we never let fear and intimidation keep us from obeying God and loving people.

WE NEED MORE HEROES. THE
WORLD DOESN'T HAVE TO BE THIS
SCARY. WE HAVE A GOD WHO HAS
OVERCOME THE WORLD, AND WE
HAVE A CHURCH CALLED TO
RESCUE IT.

CHAPTER ELEVEN
Moving Forward

Javier Botia worked as a television personality in Spain. He 'had a thriving career until one day he experienced a powerful panic attack. He canceled his show and was hospitalized twice. His doctor gave him a regimen of picking up snakes. He told him to put together a magic act for small audiences. He performed even though he wasn't that good, and it scared him. Over time, he grew in his craft and today he is an award-winning magician who travels professionally and performs all around the world. Not only did he overcome his debilitating anxiety, but he also found a new lucrative career!

Your journey may not look that dramatic. However, persistence and patience (mainly with yourself) will yield the great fruit of a courageously lived life. Life will hand you all kinds of adventures some of which may elicit anxiety, but you can live free to fulfill God's calling on your life. This chapter will give you some general principles for your forward journey.

WHO'S IN CHARGE?

Throughout this book, we've established that the key to a courageous life is keeping your most precious things in the arms of Jesus. When you give your life to God through Jesus, you establish a relationship to the Triune Godhead—the Father who loves you, Jesus who died for you, and the Spirit who guides and empowers you.

Moving forward toward a fruitful life depends upon where you place what sociologists call the "locus of control." This describes the location and essence of what you perceive controls you. Researchers have realized that people can place their locus of control in two places: internally or externally.

Someone with an external locus of control believes that most of what happens in their life depends on things outside of their control. They see themselves as a victim of circumstances and insurmountable obstacles. They somehow believe they are not in control of their lives, that fate or external forces or other people are in control and responsible.

People with an internal locus are those who believe that their life and success are up to them. They buy into the idea that although there are outside factors, they must pursue and own their future. Their theme song is, "I did it my way!" They are the "self-made men."

Those who score toward the internal end of this scale are measurably more outwardly successful in life than those who score toward the external end. They are more likely to get good jobs that they enjoy, take care of their health, and play active roles in their communities. Further, they are less likely to become anxious or depressed.

Without a relationship with God, both ways can have their downfalls. With an external locus of control, you play the victim and lose hope. You can drift into fatalism. Your victimization becomes a victim identity. There is nothing you can do so why try? You can become more susceptible to anxiety and depression. Researchers have correlated a rise in anxiety and depression with a cultural move toward an external locus of control among young people.

Tim Elmore and Barna research cited a study by Jean Twenge published a few years ago:

> Jean Twenge and her colleagues analyzed the results of several studies that used a scale based on Rotter's work (the Nowicki-Strickland Scale) with young people from 1960 through 2002. They found that over this period average scores shifted dramatically (for children aged 9 to 14 as well as for college students) away from the Internal toward the External end of the scale. In fact, the shift was so great that the average young person in 2002 was more External than 80% of young people in the 1960s. The rise in Externality on Rotter's scale over the 42-year period showed the same linear trend as did the rise in depression and anxiety. Not only do students feel that adults (not themselves) are largely in control of their lives and outcomes, but they have a phone with constant pings, rings, and pop-ups, putting them in a reactionary mode. And when people are in a reactionary mode, they tend to develop an external locus of control. [41]

An internal sense of control can drift into independence. You can think you really did do it your way. Your life can become unmoored from the grace that God and others have given you. You can even think you are your own savior. You can conclude you are the Sovereign instead of the steward and child of the Sovereign. You can gain the world and lose your soul.

41. Tim Elmore, Generation Z Unfiltered: Facing Nine Hidden Challenges of the Most Anxious Population, (Alpharetta, GA: Poet Gardner Publishing, 2019), Kindle.

WHEN WE GIVE OUR LIVES TO JESUS, THERE IS A CONVERSION EXPERIENCE, A BORN-AGAIN EXPERIENCE THAT MARRIES OUR WILL WITH THE LEADERSHIP, COUNSEL, AND EMPOWERMENT OF THE HOLY SPIRIT.

When we give our lives to Jesus, there is a conversion experience, a born-again experience that marries our will with the leadership, counsel, and empowerment of the Holy Spirit. Living with a Holy Spirit locus of control is the secret to success in every circumstance. Notice I didn't say it's the secret to a pain-free or fear-free life. No, this is the secret to a meaningful life (full of purpose), and at the end of your days, to receive a "well done" from our Lord. This is success. This becomes a journey, an adventure with God for his purposes for your life.

It gives us an identity driven by adoption into God's family; a direction led by the Spirit of God. Life happens, but it's filtered through God's hand. It's never beyond his ability to bring hope, redemption, and even good out of the bad, out-of-control, unjust, unfair circumstances in our lives.

We can be victimized but our victimization doesn't become our identity. In Christ, we become more than conquerors. I have been victimized but I am not a victim. Jesus has made me a victor—free in Christ to serve others.

At some point we have to say, yes, that was hurtful, or I got a raw deal but in Christ, my life is purposeful, and I'm going to get busy living that out. *We must recognize that the reasons for my situation do not have to be an excuse for me staying there.*

Rachel Gilson wrote the book, *Born Again This Way*, about her journey with same-sex attraction and her encounter with God and our propensity to overanalyze why we are the way we are as an excuse to stay the way we are:

And sometimes I think this is a not very helpful emphasis. Most people who experience same-sex attraction just experience it without knowing where the heck it comes from. Maybe it's partially genes—maybe it's partially environment—all the science has been done on it (emphasizes the uncertainty of its origins) is super, like we don't know exactly where it comes from. But Christians have never needed to know where something has come from to evaluate whether we should say yes to it or not. We've got the Scriptures to be able to evaluate whether I should say yes or not. I feel very secure in the fact that I experience same-sex attraction. I didn't ask for it, don't know where it came from, but it's a result of the fall, and so because I'm in Christ, I never have to say yes to it, and I have every resource possible to say no to any of the temptations that I face.[42]

With the Holy Spirit guiding our lives, he leads us to not just handle what comes but affect what is, and what will be. Empowered and led by the Spirit, we can make a difference in the lives of people for eternity! With the Holy Spirit as the navigator, our will is now guided by God to affect the destinies of those around us. When my mother at 33 years of age gave her life to Christ, it affected generations. She had no idea how God would use her life, much of it a victim of this world, to create multigenerational victors for God.

Keep communication with God through the Holy Spirit alive and current. Seek God for your goals and dreams. Read the Bible to learn about God and see where you fit into the story. Cultivate your ear to his leading: "For those who are led by the Spirit of God are the children of God" (Romans 8:14).

A few years ago, I found myself in a foreign police station threatened with punishment because of the humanitarian work our team accomplished. Some governments don't appreciate the opportunity for their people to know God through Jesus. To say I was a bit fearful might be an understatement. However, I had a peace and internal confidence because I knew the Holy Spirit had

---

42. Quoted from an interview: https://strongwomen.libsyn.com/s2-14-a-better-yes-with-rachel-gilson?_hsmi=210169094&_hsenc=p2ANqtz-_GeLTKzbfvF9EL6njdd1Y4hgTZhT8-vhUmwNBbJKh22_EJNzw7dQSiqaKPQ8YBqRzcNgfPL9FMXxXtojU68r3YZHxvRA

led our team to do what we did. Scared? You bet. At peace? Also, yes. When you place your life into the hands of God, you can trust what you have given him.

DON'T INVITE CHAOS

One evening with a new flight student (sorry Aaron) I made the decision to turn back toward the airport because the weather had worsened. Snow squalls blew over the airport creating blizzard-like conditions. Rather than waiting until they blew over, I decided to try an instrument approach into the teeth of the storm in a small two-seat aircraft, at night. I knew I had made a questionable decision when I heard an airline captain crack the radio, "Traverse City tower, anyone make it in yet?" "No one yet, we do have a Cessna on the approach though" replied the tower. The captain came back, "I'll wait to see if he makes it before we try."

My mouth dried up. I was literally scared spitless as I made every attempt to keep the plane upright in the turbulence, in the dark, in the blowing snow. I survived that encounter (in case you wondered) and I realized I had made a poor decision to try that approach. I had invited the scary into my life. Aaron became a car salesman.

Even though God will lead you into some very non-boring adventures that may induce fear, when God has led you to it, you

153

can trust he will bring you through it. However, we are all very capable of making decisions outside of God's will that can invite chaos into our lives. When we sow to the wind the Scriptures tell us, we will reap the whirlwind. When we live our lives apart from God's purposes, we diminish our capacities and things begin to break. Relationships become dramatic, our physical and emotional health fades, financial stresses mount, worry dominates, and hope hides. God has created us to live in his world. Just as he has created physical laws, he has also created moral laws. When we align our decisions with these laws, things tend to go better.

We invite chaos by ignoring reality. God created the universe to work a certain way. When we ignore this reality by flouting God's principles, ignoring wise counsel, and living selfishly, we say to chaos, "Please come and live with me."

MAKING DECISIONS

When we are young, we make critical decisions like Fruity Pebbles or Apple Jacks? Spiderman or Batman pajamas? When we grow older, our decisions will certainly affect our future. They can invite chaos or build a foundation of peace and prosperity. Life can be arranged into seven important categories where decisions make a difference in the trajectory of our lives. If you make decisions that align with how God made us, life will go better. These seven categories are:

Faith—what we believe about God influences the rest of our beliefs. If you get this one right, you will walk with peace knowing you are doing life with your Creator and sustainer.

Attitude—we choose our attitudes. If you have a good, positive outlook, it will color the rest of your decisions. A life filled with hope, faith, love, and a can-do spirit attracts peace. Winners find a way; whiners find an excuse.

Authority—authority is everywhere, and rebellion is painted as a glorious option. But rebellion steals discipline and discipline brings freedom from chaos.

Pleasure—more people are destroyed because they could not handle the pursuit of pleasure rather than the pain of adversity.

Relationships and Sex—people matter, and sex is a great gift, but a misuse of the people in our lives and the powerful, procreative gift of sex causes much pain and chaos.

Production—God made us to make a positive contribution to this world through our education, work, time, and money management. We can invite a lot of chaos into our lives by misappropriating our time and talents.

Adversity—we will all go through pain. How we handle the losses of life will make a big difference in growing bitter or better.

My life and the lives of those I've pastored can point to good decisions leading to good consequences and bad decisions leading to chaos. If you go through unsteady and chaotic seasons in life, at least know that you didn't invite them through poor decision-making. Turn to God and let him get you out of the hole. Remember, rock bottom is when you decided to stop digging and give the shovel of your life to God.

Making decisions that align with God's design won't make us immune to pain or chaos, but it certainly creates peace in our hearts and translates to a more stable life. In these chaotic times, a life built on a solid foundation will be a great billboard toward the God we serve.

GET OFF THE COUCH

Experts have found that exercise reduces anxiety in several ways. It helps to rid your body of excess adrenaline that contributes to an increase in anxiety and heightened awareness. It helps to produce endorphins that reduce pain and creates a naturally increased sense of well-being. Some have called this a "runners high." It helps to release muscle tension and relax our spirits from agitation.

Beyond exercise, there is tremendous value in finding a sport that you enjoy, particularly one that pushes you. You don't even have to be that good, but competitive activities that encourage you to explore your limits will reap tremendous benefits in a fight with anxiety and depression. My favorite two are endurance sports like triathlons and grappling (wrestling and jiu-jitsu).

First, pushing yourself past a comfort level trains your body to do what your will asks of it. When your body says, "Hey! What in the world are you doing? We should be on the couch eating ice cream!" and you tell your body, "No, we are running a few miles," this helps you understand that feelings are not your boss.

Second, if you compete, you will feel the pressure of possible failure. I remember my eighth-grade son in a wrestling tournament winning all five of his matches. The next week, he lost all five. We learned a valuable lesson—sometimes you're the windshield and sometimes you're the bug, but life goes on. Learn what you can and continue to pursue your calling.

Sports can present a microcosm of life that presents many "safe" risks. Art can do the same. Plays and recitals place pressure upon the artist. I think people (students especially) should participate in art and a sport.

Our obsession with the virtual world of video games and social media has contributed to a rise in anxiety. The sedentary challenges of our virtual world do not fully immerse us into a life that has to assess and work through real fear-inducing circumstances.

Previous generations had their leisure pastimes, but they had to produce them. They had to make the music, they had to invent the games, often in community with neighbors and family. With virtual games, we can connect without having to do the hard work of creating and learning an instrument. There is a difference in consumption and creation, and virtual community compared to real community. People do not act the same virtually as they do face-to-face.

Athletics and things like dance also give a kinesthetic benefit to learning to control your body in space. They also deliver the pleasure stimulation of speed and movement in the brain. When I game, the virtual characters simulate like I'm playing the sport, but I'm on the couch eating Cheetos.

There is much benefit to the mastery of the body through the mind. I haven't found a better way to train this process than through physical effort or artistic mastery. When I play guitar, I have a composite experience with my body, mind, and senses. I must force my fingers to work through actual pain and my brain to remember what to do. The result is music. When I play video games, I do enjoy the strategy aspect and even the social, but I don't have the physical part that I have to push through unless I'm in a gaming marathon—then I just zombie out.

HARNESS THE POWER OF MUSIC

God created the power of music to speak directly to your soul. Sounds create a tangible reaction in our minds and bodies. If someone scratches a chalkboard, how do you react? Just as unpleasant sounds can rattle the nerves, soothing sounds can do the opposite.

God loves music. He created music to surround him in heaven. The Bible has over 800 verses relating to music. The largest book of the Bible is a songbook. God created music as a powerful medium to communicate emotion and ideas.

Music has the power to focus your mind, channel your thoughts, and bypass your reason. It can speak directly to your emotions and directly to the decision-making faculties in your soul. We typically listen to music to "amuse" ourselves, to entertain ourselves, and get our minds off what we are doing or escape from our current reality. The word "amuse" comes from two words: "a" prefix means "non" or "no" and "muse" which means "to think." So literally amusement means "non-thinking." When one is "amused" they are not thinking and giving one's brain over to the power of the music. One is now caught up in the spirit and message of the music without even realizing it. The music we listen to creates a soundtrack to our lives that can help or hinder our journey of courage.

Psychologists, therapists, and neurologists utilize the power of music to help rehabilitate people with many different diagnoses from autism to stroke, or brain injuries. Dopamine is the pleasure chemical released in the brain. It provides a sense of calm, pleasure, and euphoria.

Music causes the brain to release dopamine in the amygdala. The amygdala helps us create and store emotional events in our lives. This increases the power of music as it provokes dopamine and triggers our emotions making connections to certain experiences in our life. The brain stores shortcuts to life experiences which are triggered when certain songs are played. This is why memory and music are so closely related. Harness the power of music to affirm your worth and the glory of walking with God and loving people.

WHAT ABOUT MEDICATION?

Some may frown upon the use of medication for anxiety. However, there is nothing wrong with helpful medication. Even the Apostle Paul recommended the medicinal use of wine to Timothy. However, most doctors recommend the use of the techniques mentioned in this and other books before adding medication. Each medication has potential benefits and harmful side effects.

Some research suggests that "certain medications may actually interfere with the long-term effectiveness of the most successful treatments for anxiety. That's especially true of the techniques designed to confront phobias and fears directly through exposure. If you try psychological strategies first, you very well may discover that you don't need medication . . . Many people who take medication alone experience a quick reoccurrence of symptoms when they discontinue taking medication for any reason."[43]

Smith and Elliot give a good synopsis of the ups and downs of medication. Since I am not a doctor, I quote them at length here:

> The negative side of the argument includes: Addiction: Some medications can lead to physical and/or mental dependency. Getting off those medications can be difficult, or even dangerous, if not done properly. (However, contrary to what some people think, many medications are available that do not have addictive potential.)
>
> Long-term effects: We don't really have good information on possible long-term effects with some of the newest medications. And some medications can lead to serious problems, such as diabetes and tremors.
>
> Philosophical aversions: Some people just feel strongly that they don't like to take medications. And that's okay, but only to a point.
>
> Pregnancy and breast-feeding: Only a few drugs are recommended for women who are pregnant or breast-feeding. The potential effects on the baby or fetus are just too risky for most situations.
>
> Side effects: Most medications have various side effects, such as gastrointestinal upset, headaches, dizziness, dry mouth, and sexual dysfunction. Working with your physician to find the right medication—a drug that alleviates your anxiety and doesn't cause you overly troublesome side effects—may take some time.

---

43. Elliott and Smith, *Overcoming Anxiety for Dummies*, Kindle, 158.

The upside of medications: Sometimes medications make good sense. In weighing the pros and cons, we suggest that you take a good look at the benefits that medications can offer: When serious depression accompanies anxiety, medication can sometimes provide faster relief, especially when a person feels hopeless, helpless, or suicidal.

When anxiety severely interferes with your life, medication sometimes provides relief more quickly than therapy or lifestyle changes.

Such interferences include: Panic attacks that occur frequently and cause expensive trips to the emergency room. Anxiety that feels so severe that you stop going to work or miss out on important life events. Compulsions and obsessions that take control of your life and consume large blocks of time.

When you've tried the recommendations in this book, consulted a qualified therapist, and you still suffer from excessive anxiety, medication may provide relief. If your physician tells you that your stress level must be controlled quickly to control your high blood pressure, that blood pressure medication may, in a few cases, also reduce your stress, in addition to adding a few years to your life.

When you experience a sudden, traumatic event, a brief regimen of the right medication may help you get through it. Traumas that happen to most people at one time or another include:

- The sudden death of a loved one
- An unexpected accident
- Severe illness
- An unexpected financial disaster

- A natural disaster, such as a hurricane or earthquake
- Being the victim of a serious crime
- Being the victim of terrorism[44]

Your doctor can help you navigate this decision.

DON'T BE A STRANGER

As I bring this book to a close, my prayer is that God would use this work to bring freedom to many lives. Fear can be a healthy emotion that signals danger ahead, or it can be a tyrannical slave master that debilitates your life and reduces you to a shell of the person God designed you to be. Jesus came to set captives free. "So if the Son sets you free, you will be free indeed" (John 8:36).

On April 17, 2018, twenty minutes after Southwest Airlines flight 1380 took off, the Boeing 737 experienced a catastrophic engine failure and a rapid decompression in the cabin. The aircraft instantly initiated a snap roll to the left and experienced a violent shuddering. The pilots couldn't read the instrumentation, couldn't hear each other, and couldn't breathe. Other than that, things were fine. Captain Tammie Jo Shults helped guide the

---

44. Elliott and Smith, *Overcoming Anxiety for Dummies,* Kindle, 160.

crippled aircraft to a safe landing. She became famous for her calm demeanor that came through the radio.

What people didn't know was that she faced a "good news/bad news" scenario in her mind. She concluded the bad news was that the plane would likely disintegrate in the air. The good news she said was, "This would be the day I meet my Maker." Yet the calm in her voice went viral when they released the audio of the radio calls.

How could she have peace in a situation like that? She explained, "That's when the rush stopped. I had a calm because I knew I wouldn't be meeting a stranger. I meet with him every day."

Let's be like Captain Shults. As we get to know our Maker and Father, the world can be scary, but our hearts will have discovered true peace.

I love you,

Carey

Other Publications by Carey Waldie

On this Rock

Restoring Commitment to the Local Church

If you are a Christian, you have tasted a spiritual rebirth. You were born into a spiritual, universal family called the church. He also desires to place you in a living, local, tangible version of His church that you may grow and bear fruit for Him. Without that connection, you will miss out on the full calling that God has for you. This book will take you on a journey of discovery to find your place in His redemption plan. And if you feel that He is calling you to make a change in the church you attend, this book will help you discern if and how to go about making that change for the benefit and blessing of all.

What Dad Used to Say

A father's voice. It means so much to us. The voice of a father gives roots to our identity. It establishes our place in the world. It brings wisdom, correction, and affection. As life presents its many challenges, this book is the voice of a father helping you navigate the most important decisions of your life. It's a dad helping you succeed at living your life to the fullest, navigating relationships, money, adversity, and more.

It's arranged in short chapters, each starting with a memorable "dad saying." This book gives you a voice to listen to and then you too can pass on this wisdom to the next generation. You can remember back or speak it forward "what dad used to say."

The Top 10 Things for New Christians to Understand

God has created you for a relationship with him! He has a purpose and a plan for you, but it all starts with him. The greatest decision you will ever make is whether or not you will pursue this relationship that you were designed for. If you choose to follow him, it will change your life forever. You gain the forgiveness of your sin, a restored relationship with God, and a home in heaven.

This book is designed to help you with your first steps in this new direction. It contains ten important concepts that you must understand in order to live the fruitful life a Christian should lead.

———————————

God and Your Talent

GOD
AND YOUR *Talent*
Creating Great Art for the Glory of God
Carey Waldie

In a world where solid truths about relevant topics can be hard to find. God and Your Talent provides powerful and succinct guidance for Christians looking to honor God with their artistic talent. Carey Waldie has provided a resource to help you understand who you are as a creative agent made in the image of God while drawing near to him as your creator.

Each chapter ends with discussion questions and fun exercises designed to spur creativity. it makes a great small group resource for study and interaction.

———————————

The Christian's Guide to Wealth Creation

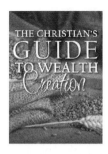

We designed this course for those who want to honor God with their talents, provide for their families, help fund the great commission and grow deeper in their relationship with the Lord.

It is a comprehensive tool that helps you learn the nature of wealth, how to create it, and how to put your money to work for you. It helps you identify and overcome obstacles to wealth creation. With nearly 30 hours of biblically balanced and economically sound instruction, we pull back the curtain on what wealth creators know but many others do not. It simplifies the often complex world investments, real estate, business ownership, IRAs and 401(k)s, and the personal and cultural characteristics that foster economic freedom and prosperity. This kit will enable you to serve others better, solve harder problems, bring order out of chaos, beauty out of ugliness, clarity out of confusion and opportunity our of emptiness. Just as God supplies the farmer with seed and we receive a harvest of bread, he is able to enlarge the storehouse of your seed so he can reap a harvest of generosity from us. If I can paraphrase the Apostle Paul's prayer for the Corinthian church, may he make you rich in every way so you can be generous on every occasion.

You will receive: 27 downloadable audio lessons with a companion ebook plus bonus materials!

Purchase via Venmo for $49.99.

————————————

Help I'm Married to the Pastor
Kimberly Waldie

"What were you ever thinking going into ministry?" As a pastor's wife, have you ever asked yourself that question? Or maybe the better question: "What was God thinking?"

Sometimes it can feel as though He made a poor choice.

Ministry life and our ever-changing culture pose a constant challenge. As pressures from church, society, and family mount, it can be a struggle for ministry couples to find joy and learn to love their role as shepherds in the body of Christ. Pastor's wives face special challenges. Too many women struggle with insecurities, fear and pain from rejection, and a burden of intimidation believing that they are making a mess of ministry life while married to the man whom they love.

Help! I'm Married to the Pastor is an authentic book of encouragement combined with a heart-felt reminder of the importance of the role of the pastor's wife. A collection of personal experiences, life-giving scripture, and practical strategies for both the newly appointed and seasoned pastor's wife, it seeks to answer the questions many pastor's wives may be afraid to ask about navigating those challenges; all the while helping them discover that there is joy to be found in serving the body of Christ.

—————————————

To order additional copies of Scared to Life, or to order other publications, please go to careywaldie.com or email cwaldie@aol.com

You may send Venmo payments to: cwaldie@aol.com

Mail Payments to:
Daniel Communications
Carey Waldie
PO BOX 452
Mayfield, MI 49666